FROM **PRISON** TO **POSSIBILITIES**

Paving Your Path

KIM NUGENT

Paperback ISBN: 978-1-960995-31-5
eBook ISBN: 978-1-960995-32-2

If you are interested in creating a Train the Trainer program , contact Kim Nugent, Ed.D at:
Email: Kim@DrNugentSpeaks.com
Website: DrNugentSpeaks.com
LinkedIn: https://www.linkedin.com/in/kimsnugent/

Cover Designs, Interior Layout & Design:
Published by Long Story Short Publishing Company in the United States of America.

DEDICATION

To Michael Bell and the Leadership Team at Management & Training Corporation,

This book is dedicated to all of you in recognition of your profound impact on prison reform. Your unwavering commitment, vision, and belief in the possibility of positive change have inspired me and countless others.

Your leadership has shown us what real prison reform looks like. From the beginning, you understood that the purpose of incarceration goes beyond punishment; it is an opportunity for rehabilitation, redemption, and, most importantly, for humanity to flourish.

Your dedication to creating an environment that fosters growth, empowers individuals, and promotes genuine transformation is commendable. You have strived to implement programs and initiatives that address the system's flaws and focus on the holistic development of incarcerated people. In doing so, you have provided hope, dignity, and a genuine chance for a better future.

Your belief that all things are possible has been a guiding light for many who have felt forgotten and overlooked. You have shown us that second chances are deserved and essential for building a more just and compassionate society. Your leadership has helped bridge the gap between incarceration and reintegration, demonstrating that individuals can overcome their past, redefine their futures, and positively contribute to their communities.

Thank you for your tireless efforts, visionary spirit, and unwavering belief in every individual's inherent worth and potential. Your commitment to real prison reform paved the way for transformation, healing, and a better world.

With profound gratitude and admiration,

Kim

TESTIMONIALS

Excellent and practical! Kim Nugent's chapters are full of thoughtful reflections on the realistic transitions people face leaving prison and offer a guide for successfully moving into a new life with opportunities for healing and growth.

–Marshall Goldsmith
Thinkers 50 no. 1 Executive Coach
and two-time no. 1 Leadership Thinker in the world

A quote that has guided me personally is, "Each new day is a new opportunity to improve yourself." I am excited for anyone reading this book because the tips and advice in these pages will undoubtedly lead to opportunities to improve yourself and help pave your pathway to success. Please know that I am rooting for you and believe in you!

–Justin K. Wood
General Counsel
Vice President of External Relations
Children's Advocacy Centers of Texas

I am very impressed with the research, content, and organization of Kim Nugent's book *From Prison to Possibilities.* As the subtitle indicates, this book outlines a path for the incarcerated to follow both in prison and after release. When studied with a capable mentor, this book provides a detailed path to enhance the probability of success in the free world. I encourage mentors to implement this book in their work with inmates and returning citizens.

–John Sage
Founder and CEO, Bridges for Life

Dr. Kim Nugent is a rare and wonderful blessing in our world—bringing a wise, practical mind and a compassionate and open heart to her work. This book is easy to comprehend yet deep and powerful in its application of the spiritual principles of transformation that have changed human lives for millennia. *From Prison to Possibilities* offers a path of hope and the steps to achieve its realization.

–Rev. Michael Gott
Senior Minister, Unity of Houston

As a leader in adult high school education, both inside and outside the prison system, I have spent years watching individuals who have been incarcerated rise to transform their lives.

The tools and support provided behind those walls is the difference maker. *From Prison to Possibilities* is a well-researched and thoughtful tool that will indeed transform lives. Dr. Nugent has developed an intentional guide for people who have been historically marginalized to flourish, marrying self-actualization, practicality, and faith into a confidence-building road map for the future.

While the workbook is easy to read and understand, the work will be challenging. Settle in, lean on your mentor, and have faith that you are worth the effort.

–Traci Berry
Education Advocate

Dr. Kim Nugent has a unique and practical approach to motivational material. Unlike so many other publications of this genre, Kim's books do not allow readers to simply sit back and read her material. Her style offers essential guidance and provides readers with exercises to apply that knowledge to their lives.

Her latest book, *From Prison to Possibilities: Paving Your Path*, provides this wisdom to a very special audience. It is focused on prisoners who are about to reenter society.

Most of us are aware of our country's high rate of recidivism. The fact that so many people return to prison proves we are doing something wrong—or not enough. Kim's approach helps them prepare for everything from filling out a job application to finding a spiritual path that will give them the support and strength to stay on track.

For the last several years, I have been involved with prison officials and the people residing there. I have reviewed a great deal of material on this subject. But I have yet to find anything as focused and on target as Kim's latest work, *Prison to Possibilities: Paving Your Path*.

–Bill DeBarba
Author and Speaker, *The Process of Living*

CONTENTS

PURPOSE

To help inmates successfully transition from incarceration to living a full life post-release by the following:

- Identifying key traits to work on prior prerelease
- Developing a plan for post-release
- Creating a pathway for transition
- Providing a mentoring ministry approach
- Reducing recidivism (the chances of returning to prison)

INTRODUCTION

This book aims to develop a plan for your successful transition from incarceration to living a full and productive life post-release. Ideally, the process of getting ready for the transition starts thirty weeks before your release. The ideal structure is for you to have a mentor go through this program every week for twenty-six weeks while still in prison and obtain an external mentor twelve weeks post-incarceration. The objective is to reduce recidivism by addressing community-reintegration issues and providing a structure for transition success. In other words, to keep you from returning to prison by helping you build a successful life as you address typical problems in the free world outside of the prison walls.

By the grace of God, most people have not been incarcerated and probably cannot imagine how their life would have turned out if they had gone to prison. I pray that if you or your family member or a church partner are reading this book, they will believe you are worth it and want to reinvest in you to give you a second chance. We all deserve a second chance. Indeed, God has provided for a lifetime of opportunities.

I also pray that you have taken advantage of all the programs that prison offers and that it has changed you for the better. Some prisons have very innovative programs and are committed to reducing recidivism, and we applaud them. These include staffing agencies to help with employment, the ability to obtain a GED, a high school diploma, and community college credits to learn a trade or obtain a certification. Some prisons offer meditation, yoga, substance-abuse programs, counseling, weight training, and basketball to advance mental and physical well-being. In some very special prisons, programs include animal husbandry, farming, fostering dogs, and dog training, leading to employment post-release.

Faith-based programs like Bridges to Life, Mike Barber Ministries, and Kairos Ministry have made great strides in partnering with prisons and inmates to help healing begin.

Bridges to Life is a faith-based restorative justice program for incarcerated men and women that provides a platform for life-changing transformation. The organization was founded by John Sage in 1998 out of an unspeakable tragedy: the murder of John's sister, Marilyn, in 1993. John realized through his and his family's suffering, it had also impacted friends, coworkers, and the community. John began volunteering for a prison ministry where crime victims shared their stories with offenders and saw the compassion awakened to the impact of their actions. The spiritual mission of Bridges to Life is to minister to victims and offenders to show them the transforming power of God's love and forgiveness.

While volunteering in prisons, I had the opportunity to speak with men and women about the impact of the Bridges to Life program. Each person shared how going through the fourteen-week program and confronting their actions enabled them to hold themselves accountable, confess, and achieve true forgiveness for the first time. In our conversations, you could sense inner peace. They felt a renewed sense of how their life could be different post-release.

Kairos Ministry is a Christian faith-based ministry that addresses the spiritual needs of incarcerated men, women, youth, and their families. By sharing the love and forgiveness of Jesus Christ, Kairos hopes to change hearts, transform lives, and impact the world. The word *kairos* is a Greek word meaning "in God's special time."

Many inmates pre- and post-incarceration have shared their stories with me. I have a whole new appreciation for the meaning of the word *kairos*. Each person shared that while Kairos had a powerful and visible presence in their prison, it would take them many years to participate. Some stayed away for years out of fear of the gang they were in and what might happen. Some family members encouraged them to join, and they ignored them for years until, one day, they couldn't. Some joined out of curiosity, and maybe some just signed up for the home-baked cookies. Regardless, over a weekend, their lives were transformed. What is most impressive is that many of these same individuals continue to serve in the ministry post-release because of the impact made in their lives.

Mike Barber Ministries is a Christian-based organization committed to presenting salvation and spiritual renewal through Jesus Christ to men and women behind bars. I was invited to participate in one of those weekends, which was life changing for me. I can only imagine what it was like for the incarcerated participants.

The entire Barber family is committed to making a difference in the life of each person they minister to, which includes men and women behind bars, the prison staff, the volunteers, and the entire team that supports the organization. Not surprisingly, some of the volunteers who had been incarcerated and released returned to volunteer to minister to others and let them know they are not forgotten.

The Barber Ministry's love and commitment to allow people to see what is possible through Jesus Christ is inspiring. I had the opportunity to witness baptisms, participate in the music and ministry program, meet great people, and even visit death row. I noticed that the people who had or did accept Jesus Christ into their hearts were changed. In some cases, the people in prison are freer than people on the outside who are imprisoned in their minds. While my commitment was strong to be effective through this mentoring program, their passion reignited my passion to do even more.

You might be wondering why I would write a book like this. When I was a teenager, my dad became a criminal attorney at 40. Before he married my mom, my dad went to the Catholic seminary for six years and fell ill one year before being ordained. He recovered while back home and ended up getting married and having six children. He was an interesting man to watch. Despite dealing with many illnesses throughout his life, he had an incredible work ethic. Each day when he went to the office or the courthouse, he had an unshakable belief that all people were innocent until proven guilty, and that is how he served as an attorney for thirty years.

When I was 18 years old, I went to work for a bail bonding company for a year, working the 11:00 p.m. to 7:00 a.m. shift. I saw the inner workings of the city and county jail and the state prison in Texas. When my brother Geff turned 21, he became a Houston police officer. He truly wanted to make a difference in the lives of others. Family dinners were interesting, as I'm sure you can imagine. No matter what role any of my brothers or sisters chose, we knew our purpose was to make a difference in the lives of others. It was the way we were raised. Little did I know how my life would change almost 40 years later.

One day, I received a phone call from a gentleman named Bill DeBarba from Arizona. He volunteered in prisons doing mediation workshops. He knew I had written a book on mentorship and asked if I would be willing to write a book on mentorship for incarcerated men and women. He saw a real need for guidance, direction, and connection. I said yes. The book research began, and the rest is history.

NOTHING BUT THE FACTS

Did you know inmates who participate in correctional education programs have 43 percent lower odds of returning to prison (S. Davis et al. 2014, 18)? More than 2 million adults are incarcerated in the United States. More than 700,000 incarcerated individuals leave federal and state prisons each year, and within three years of release, over 40 percent return to prison. There are many reasons for this. For some individuals, it is a lack of necessary education to find secure employment. For some, it is a literacy issue. For many, it is a substance-abuse issue.

Without a comprehensive plan and educational programs in place, it is a dismal situation. Fortunately, many new opportunities are available to begin to change this cycle. While it starts with prison administrators being open to sharing best practices and researching recent trends, the ultimate ownership belongs to each incarcerated individual, who must decide what path to take and how to help themselves while in prison so they do not return. *Whatever got you into prison, returning to that environment will send you right back!*

Whatever you have imagined freedom will be like, think again. It will be more challenging than you ever imagined. There are things they do not tell you or prepare you for about reintegration, and you will need a new set of life skills to be successful.

Living in a prison is hard. Every decision is made for you—when you get up, where you can walk, what time to eat, the uniform to wear, where to report to work, when you can call, when to go to bed, etc.

When you are out, very few decisions will be made for you; they will be yours. You might fantasize about what you will do when you first get out. For many, it is just getting out of prison, walking in the sunshine, and getting picked up and brought home. If you are fortunate, it might happen. Once you get home, you want to shower, sit, eat a home-cooked meal, and get reacquainted with family and friends. You want to sleep in your old bed. Maybe you will adjust or not. Perhaps you have gotten so used to the prison sounds, lights, and environment that you can't sleep. That could be a real surprise.

What you imagined freedom looks like will last maybe three days, and then reality will slip in. It might be a comment like, "It's nice you are home. When are you going to find a job? Pay rent? Take care of the children? Cook? Stop hanging out with the people who caused you problems in the first place? Manage your addictions?" In prison, decisions were made for you. Now personal responsibility and decision-making have set in.

Release from prison can pose unique challenges for women to transition successfully. Here are some potential questions and issues to consider:

How are you going to rebuild support systems?
Women may struggle to reconnect with family, friends, or community members who have distanced themselves during incarceration. Helping them rebuild and strengthen their support networks can be crucial.

How do you create financial stability?
Finding employment and securing a stable income is often a significant concern for women after prison. They may need job placement, vocational training, or financial planning assistance to regain financial independence. Non-profit organizations such as Career Recovery Resources may provide the resources to get you started.

Where can you find stable housing?
Many women leaving incarceration lack suitable housing arrangements, hindering their reintegration into society. Ensuring access to safe and stable housing can significantly impact their successful transition. Organizations like the Star of Hope may be able to help with temporary housing.

Am I dealing with mental health and trauma issues?
Women who have been incarcerated may have experienced traumatic events or may struggle with mental health issues, which require support and special resources. Organizations like the National Alliance for Mental Illness can provide access to counseling, therapy, and other mental health services essential to staying healthy.

Am I prepared to positively parent and reconnect with my family and children?
Women who are mothers face the challenge of reconnecting with their children and rebuilding relationships that may have been strained during their incarceration. Family support services and parenting programs can be valuable resources in this process. What resources in prison can I take advantage of, such as Acceleron Learning to prepare for reentry?

How do I plan to address substance use and addiction issues when I am released? Substance use issues are prevalent among incarcerated women. Upon release, they may require support and access to programs that aid in addiction recovery and rehabilitation. If part of the reason there is an addiction issue is you were introduced to drugs and alcohol by a boyfriend or partner, being able to leave that relationship to maintain sobriety will be required. Can you do that?

How have you prepared yourself to reenter the job market while in prison?
Women may face additional obstacles when reentering the workforce due to gaps in employment history, stigma associated with incarceration, and difficulty securing necessary identification documents. Providing career counseling, job training, and assistance with job applications can be crucial.

How have you improved building life skills?
Helping women develop essential life skills such as budgeting, time management, conflict resolution, and decision-making will support successful reintegration into society.

Be prepared to be patient rather than respond in anger when dealing with legal and bureaucratic barriers. Be willing to ask for help. Formerly incarcerated women can encounter administrative issues related to probation or parole, restoration of voting rights, child custody matters, etc. Assisting them in navigating these legal challenges can enable a smoother transition.

You are unique. It is important to note that the specific challenges women face transitioning from incarceration may vary. Individualized support and a holistic approach that addresses their individual needs can significantly enhance their chances of successful reentry into society.

How will you cope? Start thinking now about what you need, what you will do to change, and who the people are to walk alongside you and help. Start thinking about surrounding yourself with positive people who want to see you succeed, not people who want to keep you down. Who are the people and the situations you need to avoid? What places do you need to avoid? What habits do you need to stop? Let's get started.

CHARACTER STRENGTHS: WHO ARE YOU?

Before we embark on paving a new path and looking for new possibilities, we must determine a baseline of where you are today. In this chapter, take the time to self-reflect before working with a mentor. Being incarcerated is a traumatic event that can have many adverse effects.

Specific character strengths can help you build a strong foundation. They are responsibility, gratitude, honesty, forgiveness, self-regulation, self-worth, and spirituality. The definition of each word follows:

- o   Responsibility is for you to state the actions where you were at fault or in the wrong.
- o   Gratitude is being thankful and your ability to show appreciation.
- o   Honesty is the ability to tell the truth.
- o   Forgiveness is a process of forgiving and/or being forgiven.
- o   Self-regulation is the ability to control your emotions and actions, set long-lasting goals, and achieve them.
- o   Self-worth is the ability to appreciate your uniqueness and potential.
- o   Faith is the quality of being concerned about the human spirit or soul. It is your relationship with your Creator and finding your purpose in life.

According to social psychologist James Pennebaker of the University of Texas at Austin, writing about the events that have happened to you in your life can help you let go and heal in various ways (E. E. Smith 2017, 171–173). First, look at the causes and consequences of what happened to you. Write out how you feel. Hold nothing back. Go ahead and get started before you even meet with your mentor. Instructions are on the next page.

Writing Exercise

Each day, take fifteen minutes and write at least one page to think about the character strengths listed. Do not worry about grammar, spelling, punctuation, etc. The goal is to get your thoughts on paper.

Responsibility. What happened that caused you to be incarcerated? Have you taken responsibility for your choices? What have your actions cost your family?

Thought starters on responsibility:

I am incarcerated because…

My earliest memory of getting into trouble was…

The impact of my crime on the victim is…

The impact on my family is…

I am taking responsibility for…

Writing Exercise

Each day, take fifteen minutes and write at least one page to think about the character strengths listed. Do not worry about grammar, spelling, punctuation, etc. The goal is to get your thoughts on paper.

Gratitude. Are you showing gratitude each day?

Thought starters on gratitude:

I am grateful for…

A person I am grateful for because of their positive influence in my life is…

What I have learned from this is…

Writing Exercise

Each day, take fifteen minutes and write at least one page to think about the character strengths listed. Do not worry about grammar, spelling, punctuation, etc. The goal is to get your thoughts on paper.

Honesty. Are you able to tell the truth? Do you know the difference between honesty and your opinion?

Thought starters on honesty:

I tell the truth about…

I tell the truth to myself about…

I tell the truth to my family…

I tell the truth to…

I lie about…

Truth is different from my opinion.

My opinion is…

But the truth is…

Writing Exercise

Each day, take fifteen minutes and write at least one page to think about the character strengths listed. Do not worry about grammar, spelling, punctuation, etc. The goal is to get your thoughts on paper.

Forgiveness. Have you forgiven yourself and asked for forgiveness?

Thought starters on forgiveness:

Programs I have taken in prison to learn about forgiveness are…

I have forgiven…

Do you believe God has forgiven you? If yes, explain your reasons.

I have forgiven myself for…

Writing Exercise

Each day, take fifteen minutes and write at least one page to think about the character strengths listed. Do not worry about grammar, spelling, punctuation, etc. The goal is to get your thoughts on paper.

Self-regulation. Are you able to control your emotions and recognize emotional triggers?

Thought starters on self-regulation:

Emotional triggers for me are…

I can control my triggers by …

I still find it difficult to…

Writing Exercise

Each day, take fifteen minutes and write at least one page to think about the character strengths listed. Do not worry about grammar, spelling, punctuation, etc. The goal is to get your thoughts on paper.

Self-worth. What do you value about your life?

Thought starters on self-worth:

The people I matter to the most are…

I value….

I am unique…

What is special about you?

Writing Exercise

Each day, take fifteen minutes and write at least one page to think about the character strengths listed. Do not worry about grammar, spelling, punctuation, etc. The goal is to get your thoughts on paper.

Faith. Who are *you*? What do you believe in? What do you value? What is your purpose? Have you found a higher power to believe in? Do you do your best to practice your faith daily?

Thought starters on faith:

I am…

I believe in…

I value…

My purpose in life is…

My faith allows me to…

For me, faith means….

List the characteristics of faith and spirituality:

To experience real growth, Pennebaker has found in his research that people who have experienced a traumatic event and can write about it function better. As your perspective changes from writing these things out, Pennebaker suggests finding positive meaning in your traumatic experience. Finding positive meaning will bring growth. This will take time. These writing exercises can be done daily on your own. While in prison, we hope you take advantage of the educational and faith-based programs the prison offers. It is time to prepare for the future.

THE EDUCATION PATHWAYS

Many prison programs offer opportunities for incarcerated men and women to change the course of their futures with educational programs. There has been a lot of research by the Bureau of Justice Assistance and the RAND Corporation on the relationship between correctional education, employment, and recidivism. In addition, the Bureau of Labor Statistics shares the impact of education on future earnings every year. The bottom line is the more you learn, the more you earn, and unemployment rates are reduced.

Prison programs have offered inmates the opportunity to earn a GED for years. Some prison systems allow inmates to acquire a GED, such as the Windham School District (WSD) in Texas. Windham provides appropriate educational programs to meet the needs of the eligible offender population, thus reducing recidivism by assisting offenders in becoming productive members of society.

In addition, in Texas, the legislature changed the law to allow adults to earn a high school diploma from eighteen to fifty. The Goodwill Excel Centers are a unique tuition-free charter high school that awards certifications and diplomas for adult learners in some local communities. The Goodwill Excel Center, located in Austin, Texas, serves adult learners in the community and has high school programs in several prisons throughout Texas.

Some prison systems have partnered with the local community college to allow inmates to earn college credit in prison so they have a brighter future upon release.

Depending on the prison system, many have incorporated some trades to operate within the prison so incarcerated men and women can go through an apprenticeship and learn a trade. Other prison systems offer certifications in high-demand fields to allow inmates to earn more upon release.

In addition, some innovative prison systems have partnered with businesses and industries to offer programs, including manufacturing, light industrial, hydro blasting, CDL drivers, mechanics, food service, light clerical, and culinary. The intention is for inmates to be able to use those skills upon release and earn a living wage.

Some prisons offer a Prison Entrepreneurship Program (PEP) with volunteers as servant leaders on a mission to transform inmates and executives by unlocking God-given potential through entrepreneurial passion, education, and mentoring. The program provides resources and real-world value-based business skills to inmates so they have the skills and support to live productive lives once they are back in society. While in prison, inmates learn how to develop a business plan and a marketing plan, then promote the idea prelease and hopefully open their own business.

While you have choices inside and outside prison, without a well-conceived plan, the odds are high that you will return to prison. This book is intended to provide a pathway that does not lead back to incarceration, but that is up to you. No one can be successful alone, so take the next step in your growth and development by choosing a mentor.

MENTORING: WHO IS GOING TO HELP YOU?

> *A mentor is not someone who walks ahead of us to show us how they did it. A mentor is someone who walks alongside us to show us what we can do.*
> —Simon Sinek

Mentors are the types of role models who can positively influence your character. According to the website Mentoring Complete (https://www.management-mentors.com), mentoring is a trustworthy professional relationship in which an experienced person (mentor) assists the mentee (you, the learner) in developing skills and knowledge to enhance the learner's professional and personal goal development (p.1). It can be one of the most valuable learning experiences for both the mentee and mentor at various points in life.

Mentoring is a pivotal component to benefit from the book fully. For this book, this mentoring relationship will last about nine months.

The structure will include an agreed-upon schedule set up weekly either via telephone, face-to-face, or technology such as Zoom if accessible. The mentor and mentee are expected to come to each session having read the prerequisite material. The mentee will be expected to complete the questions provided each week. The mentor will ask weekly questions and take notes for follow-up, next steps, and what has been learned. Because of the classroom and schedule constraints in prison, the time and date of each weekly session must be agreed upon from the beginning.

When choosing your mentor, think about whom you admire and trust, who motivates you, who speaks positively about others, and who you would be comfortable speaking with each week. A mentor is a trustworthy adult, such as a teacher, coach, advisor, counselor, family friend, or church volunteer who can be trusted and admired. It is not someone from your past who has negative traits or cannot be trusted.

This book can be used in a variety of ways such as a peer mentorship program, a church-based ministry program, or with a mentor who is a professional on staff.

Peer Mentoring

One of the most effective approaches to mentoring in prison is creating a peer mentoring program. The benefits, include:

1. Rehabilitation: Peer mentoring programs can provide an opportunity for individuals who have successfully reintegrated into society after incarceration to support and guide their fellow inmates. This can contribute to the rehabilitation process and reduce rates of recidivism by providing positive role models and support networks.
2. Empowerment: Peer mentoring programs empower incarcerated individuals by promoting personal growth, self-esteem, and a sense of purpose. It allows them to take on leadership roles, develop mentoring skills, and engage in meaningful activities that can lead to personal transformation.
3. Support and Guidance: Inmates often face various social, emotional, and psychological challenges during their incarceration. Peer mentors can provide emotional support, practical advice, and guidance on coping mechanisms, educational opportunities, job skills training, and soft skills and personal development.
4. Peer Connection: Peer mentoring programs foster a sense of community and connection among inmates. In a prison environment, this can alleviate feelings of isolation, loneliness, and hopelessness. By forming positive relationships, inmates may experience improved mental well-being and reduce their risk of engaging in negative behaviors.
5. Improved Reentry: Peer mentoring programs can enhance the successful reentry process by providing ongoing support and mentorship during the transitional period from incarceration to community. Peer mentors can help with navigating employment opportunities, housing, healthcare, and accessing additional resources needed to reintegrate effectively into society.
6. Cost Reduction: By promoting successful reintegration and reducing recidivism rates, peer mentoring programs can potentially lead to cost savings for the criminal justice system. This is because fewer individuals returning to incarceration means lower expenses related to new trials, imprisonment, probation, and associated services.

It's important to note that the effectiveness of peer mentoring programs in prisons may vary depending on various factors such as program design, training, and ongoing support for mentors. Regular evaluation and monitoring can help ensure the program's continued success and impact.

We recommend starting with an intact group such as the faith-based unit, a reentry group or other program group that is working with a curriculum before considering other groups for a pilot program.

Once you have identified the group of mentors and the initial incarcerated men or women who want the program, mentors should participate in a formal mentor training program to help them understand expectations, curriculum, training, and meeting schedule.

Then the prison leader assigned to oversee the program will work with mentors to set up to work in small groups of mentees (one to four) for approximately sixty to ninety minutes.

If you are interested in hosting a Train the Trainer program, contact Kim Nugent @ Kim@ drnugentspeaks.com or nugent1234@gmail.com

Mentoring ChurchMinistry

Most prisons have church partners who regularly serve incarcerated people in various ways: teaching, volunteering, and offering prayer support. Church volunteers who serve as mentors help incarcerated men and women successfully transition back into the community, by:

1. Support and Encouragement: An assigned mentor from a church community can provide regular support, encouragement, and motivation during and after release, helping the recently released individuals avoid feelings of loneliness, frustration, and despair.
2. Positive Role Model: A church volunteer mentor can serve as a positive role model by setting an example of positive behavior, values, and spiritual guidance, which can be beneficial for individuals trying to turn their life towards positive change.
3. Accountability: Mentors can hold individuals accountable for their actions, helping them to make better choices and avoid mistakes that could lead to re-incarceration.
4. Life Skills Training: Mentors can provide guidance and support in building important life skills such as financial management, career planning, healthy life choices, and even spiritual guidance, helping individuals transition smoothly to community living.
5. Networking: Through their involvement with the church community, mentors can help their mentees forge important connections, including job opportunities, education resources, finding a church home, and other community services.
6. Sense of Purpose: Helping others can be incredibly rewarding. Mentoring provides volunteers with a sense of purpose and a chance to give back to their community, while also helping to reduce recidivism.

    While mentoring is not a silver bullet solution for helping to reintegrate returning citizens into society, it can be a valuable part of the support system necessary for success. A mentor who is understanding, non-judgmental, and patient can be an excellent resource and support in this process of reintegration.

We hope that church partners will adopt this approach and serve as mentors. This model can be used one-on-one, or a mentor can serve up to four mentees. Given the new environment we are living through, one new solution could be using web-based technology such as Zoom to provide outreach. Regardless of who serves as a mentor, our primary goal is to offer a six-month framework to work on various skills prerelease with the mentee so they are better prepared to leave prison and not return. The secondary goal is to support the mentee in creating a realistic three-month post-release plan. This secondary mentor ideally would be a part of your church home.

MENTOR SELF-ASSESSMENT: ARE YOU READY TO BE A MENTOR?

Mentoring aims to provide an inmate with a road map pre and post-release. You will be drawing from personal career experience and professional excellence. Feedback and coaching skills are secondary.

1. What is your *why* or *purpose* for being a mentor?

2. Conduct a SOAR analysis as a mentor for yourself.

   My strengths are

   My opportunities are

   My aspirations are

   The results I want to achieve are

3. Motivation

   - What is motivating you to take on a mentoring relationship?
   - What is your vision of the best possible outcome?
   - What are your strengths in undertaking this change?
   - What obstacles might prevent you from reaching the mentee's goal?
   - Have you completed the security training program?
   - Can you commit to the weekly schedule and preparation necessary?

- List the action steps for how you will

  - Communicate
  - Use your personal experience
  - Adapt resources to the mentee's learning style
  - Deal with resistance
  - Be involved

- What new skills, knowledge, and attitudes are needed to make this change?

  - Skills
  - Knowledge
  - Attitudes

- Determine how you will acknowledge, recognize, and celebrate after the program.
- How will you keep the momentum?

4. Goal setting

- What are the mentee's personal goals upon post-release?
- What is the mentee's motivation for turning their life around?
- Once the mentee knows the pathway post-release, how will you assist in helping them complete the deliverables from the checklist?

5. Initial conversation starters

- How is it going?
- What did you accomplish this week?
- What did you learn about yourself this week?
- Catch me up.

6. For this relationship to be productive, getting to know your mentee is essential.

- Communication strategies:

  - Build connections and trust.
  - Be empathetic.
  - Use active listening.
  - Explore options. There is plenty of time.
  - Encourage.
  - Know the resources and programs the prison has available.
  - Co-create opportunities.
  - Acknowledge the effort they are putting in.
  - Do not violate prison regulations and overstep.

- Facilitating/asking questions: The great thing about this book is the questions have been created for you. You can certainly expand on them. We want to caution you on what is not helpful regarding your approach. We have found these approaches are not useful in the mentoring relationship.

Remember:

- You are not a therapist.
- Be a friend first before being a mentor. Developing a strong bond of trust is critical.
- Telling them everything you have done for the past twenty to forty years is not the focus.
- Asking questions is most helpful in this relationship. Sometimes, inmates are looking for answers, and that is when your experience can help guide them.
- Do not push your agenda.
- Do not solve their problems. The mentee needs to solve the problem for themselves. If there is a week when you feel the mentee is going in the wrong direction, pause the conversation. Ask the mentee to write their thoughts about what they want to accomplish and pick it up next week. You both need time to reflect. Don't push it if it does not feel right.
- Do not tell them what to do.

Feedback

- Don't ask "why" questions. It puts people on the defensive, and behaviors do not change. Once a relationship is established, your questions will come naturally.
- Begin discussions with "how" or "what" questions.
- Always be respectful of your mentee.
- Actively listen to what is being said.

7. Problem-solving. Use this model to problem solve. (Connellan 2002, *Bringing Out the Best in Others*).

- Define the issue.
- Explore options.
- Develop solutions.
- Reinforce positive ideas.
- Close the deal/gain agreements. Don't assume anything; ask for their commitment.

8. Reflection on learning

- How are you doing?
- What is working?
- Where are you struggling, or is there anything you are confused about?

9. Structure

- Commit once a week to meet. Be flexible.
- Phone, face-to-face, or web-based technology if allowed.
- Set time and date.
- Take notes.

10. Celebrate learning/rewards:

- Thank-you notes
- Face-to-face acknowledgment

The research is evident that having a mentor in life is very helpful. While many organizations start mentoring programs, the programs typically do not produce the intended result or merely do not remain active. Preparation is vital to prevent this from happening.

Preparation and expectations for the mentor:

- Review and commit to the schedule.
- Read the chapter/article for the week.
- Review the self-assessment questions.
- Review the mentor questions.
- Look ahead to next week so you are clear about expectations.
- Think about how you can expand the conversation based on the goals and your experience. Feel free to bring in additional resources.

> *People will forget what you said, people will forget what you did, but people will never forget how you made them feel.*
> —Maya Angelou

MENTEE-MENTOR AGREEMENT

We are both excited about embarking on this journey together. We both want this to be a rewarding experience, spending most of our time discussing developmental activities that will provide valuable knowledge in the future. We agree on the following:

1. The mentoring relationship will last up to nine months. If it does not meet the mentee's needs for some reason, we can decide to end the formal relationship at any time through a conversation. In some formal programs sponsored by the prison, it is possible to have two mentors, one mentor for using this book for six months and an external mentor for three months post-release to ensure you are working on your post-release plan and know how to access resources to prevent returning to prison.
2. We will meet once a week via Zoom. Meeting times, once agreed, should not be canceled unless unavoidable. At the end of each meeting, we will agree on a date for the next meeting.
3. Plan on each meeting lasting sixty (60) minutes, but the mentor and mentee(s) should choose what is best for both parties. The prison will use their Zoom account and schedule the room, time, and day of the week. Schedule for 1.5 hours to allow the mentees to leave their housing area and be escorted to the classroom.
4. We agree that the role of the mentor is as follows:
   - Take the online security training course and pass it before becoming approved.
   - Provide guidance, share ideas, and provide feedback.
   - Act as a sounding board for ideas/concerns about life choices.
   - Know what resources are available at the prison.
   - Identify resources to help enhance personal development and career growth.
   - Serve as an advocate for the mentee whenever the opportunity presents itself.
   - The goal is to co-create a realistic post-release plan with the mentee.

5. We agree that the role of the mentee (you, the learner) is as follows:
   - Identify the skills, knowledge, and/or goals you want to achieve and communicate with your mentor.
   - Maintain a mentoring plan and work with your mentor to set goals, developmental activities, and time frames.
   - Work with your mentor to see resources for learning. Identify people and information that might be helpful.
   - The goal is to create a realistic post-release plan you are comfortable with.

6. We agree to keep the content of these meetings confidential.

7. The mentor agrees to be honest and provide constructive feedback to the mentee. The mentee agrees to be open to feedback and say thank you.

Date:_____

Mentor's signature: _____

Mentee's signature: _____

Format

Weekly sessions can be taught face to face (peer mentoring) or using zoom or web-based technology (church ministry approach) would be ideal if the prison allows technology. It can also allow a mentor to mentor up to four mentees.

Train the Trainer

A Train the Trainer program is available for mentors, so they feel confident in the approach and expected outcomes. Contact Kim Nugent at Kim@drnugentspeaks.com or nugent1234@gmail.com

GETTING TO KNOW YOU GUIDE

Mentee Name:

Before we get started, let's get to know each other. We need to examine if you are in a growth mindset and want to take on having a mentor. By answering each of these questions, you will begin to review your skills, traits, competencies, and abilities before using the self-assessment guide for each of the 26 traits.

Tell me a little about yourself.

What did you learn through the writing activity on character strengths?

Are you motivated to leave prison? If yes, what are the reasons?

After the 26 weeks, what do you want to accomplish?

What programs have you taken advantage of while in prison?

How do you learn best?

_____Auditory
_____Visual
_____Tactile-Kinesthetic

What are three of your strengths?
1.

2.

3.

What are three of your weaknesses?
1.

2.

3.

What is your personality style?

What do you do for your health and well-being?

How do you solve problems?

What assistance do you need in overcoming obstacles?

What were the last three books you read?

Do you want a mentor?

Are you willing to participate fully in this weekly program and do the work?

Our weekly schedule will be held on _____(day) and _____(time).

Thank you for completing the Getting to Know You Guide.

PRE-RELEASE PATHWAY TO READINESS: SELF-AWARENESS

On Becoming More Self-Aware—Inventory Instructions

Self-Awareness

What if we created a win-win situation? Let's begin by starting the self-assessment inventory. Please take it before you start on this journey. Let's determine how self-aware you are at this point. Let's get started.

Pre-Self-Assessment Inventory

ABCs from Prison to Possibility	At the beginning of the program, rate yourself from 1 to 10 (1 being poor and 10 being excellent).	Plan to improve/Resources utilized
A is for *attitude*. Show a positive attitude.		
B is for *behavior*. What behavior do you want to work on first?		
C is for *communication*. Be a good communicator.		
D is for *decision-making*. Improve your decision-making skills.		
E is for *emotional intelligence*. Can you keep your emotions under control?		

ABCs from Prison to Possibility	At the beginning of the program, rate yourself from 1 to 10 (1 being poor and 10 being excellent).	Plan to improve/Resources utilized
F is for *finance*. Become skilled at handling your money.		
G is for *goal setting*. Focus on the most important goals.		
H is for *health*. Think about your current state of health and well-being.		
I is for *integrity*. Maintain your word to yourself and others. Can others trust you 100 percent?		
J is for *Jesus*. Stand up for what you believe in.		
K is for *knowledgeable*. Expand your knowledgebase.		
L is for *lifelong learning*. Hold yourself accountable for lifelong learning.		
M is for *mindset*. Explore. Do you learn from your mistakes?		
N is for *new media literacy*. Are you skilled in using new media?		
O is for *opportunity*. Actively look for new life opportunities and take appropriate and legal risks.		

ABCs from Prison to Possibility	At the beginning of the program, rate yourself from 1 to 10 (1 being poor and 10 being excellent).	Plan to improve/Resources utilized
P is for *PTSD* (post-traumatic stress disorder). Understand your triggers and learn strategies that work.		
Q is for *questioning*. Become more curious by asking questions.		
R is for *resiliency*. Do you adapt or just give up?		
S is for *self-awareness*. Increase your self-awareness.		
T*hank you*. Show thankfulness and gratitude.		
U is for *understanding*. Learn to listen to others' points of view before sharing yours.		
V is for *victory*. Do you celebrate victories for yourself and others?		
W is for *work*. How strong is your work ethic?		
X—*cultural competency*. Appreciate and respect differences in other races and cultures.		
Y is for *your network*. Work with others and build your support group.		
Z is for *zealous*. Expand opportunities for bringing enthusiasm to your life.		

INSTRUCTIONS FOR THE MENTOR

Welcome to the Mentor Facilitation Workshop Schedule

Program Orientation

Forms

      Book Review

      Self-Reflection Writing Activities

      Getting to Know You Guide

      Mentor Agreement

      Weekly Schedule Day/Time/Location

      Pre-Self-Assessment

      A – Z Weekly Articles/Questions

Set the weekly schedule and provide your contact information to the prison staff scheduler.

Set the time. Schedule 1.5 hours to allow the men or women to get to the classroom. Know the meeting may be delayed because of getting the mentees to the classroom and other priorities in the prison. You only need 1 hour per week for each session. You will mentor a small group of 1 to 4 people.

Share the weekly expectations with your mentees. You and the mentees must be prepared to read the article, answer the questions, and participate weekly in the discussion. Some weeks will require more homework as you start preparing the post-release plan.

The Weekly Schedule by Topic

Week	Mentor Topics	Assignments for the Next Week
Week 1	Getting to Know You Guide	Read pages 1-34.
Week 2	Self-Reflection: Discuss the Self-Reflection section.	Read 32-42. Complete the Self-Assessment Inventory, read A is for Attitude, and complete the mentee questions.
Week 3	A is for Attitude Discuss the article and ask the mentor questions.	
Week 4	B is for Behavior Discuss the article and ask the mentor questions.	Behavior-based questions start as a daily practice for accountability.
Week 5	C is for Communication Discuss the article and ask the mentor questions.	
Week 6	D is for Decision Making Discuss the article and ask the mentor questions.	
Week 7	E is for Emotional Intelligence Discuss the article and ask the mentor questions.	
Week 8	F is for Finance Discuss the article and ask the mentor questions. Develop a plan for post-release.	
Week 9	G is for Goal Setting Discuss the article and ask the mentor questions.	
Week 10	H is for Health Discuss the article and ask the mentor questions.	
Week 11	I is for Integrity Discuss the article and ask the mentor questions.	

Week	Mentor Topics	Assignments for the Next Week
Week 12	J is for Jesus Discuss the article and ask the mentor questions.	
Week 13	K is for Knowledge Discuss the article and ask the mentor questions. Review the Career Development Tools section.	Read the Career Development Tool Section. Complete the following: Application Exercise Functional Resume Proof of Education/Certifications Create a list of Recommendations/References
Week 14	L is for Learning Review the Appendix and Resources at the end of the book (pages 179-180) to see what resources you need that you do not have yet. Begin working to obtain them.	Read the section on Now Hired, Now What?
Week 15	M is for Mindset Discuss the article and ask the mentor questions. Discuss Now Hired, Now What? Meet the post-release mentor virtually (initial meet and greet is done with the current mentor).	
Week 16	N is for New-Media Literacy O is for Opportunity Discuss the articles and ask the mentor questions.	
Week 17	P is for PTSD Discuss the article and ask the mentor questions.	

Week	Mentor Topics	Assignments for the Next Week
Week 18	Q is for Questioning Discuss the article and ask the mentor questions.	Read the Career Development Section about: Personal Hygiene Handshake Punctuality Interviewing The Challenging Questions Be ready to practice the interview questions.
Week 19	R is for Resiliency Discuss the article and ask the mentor questions. Discuss the Career Development assignment from last week.	
Week 20	S is for Spirituality Discuss the article and ask the mentor questions. Meet potential mentor post-release and touch base.	
Week 21	T is for Thank You U is for Understanding Discuss the articles and ask the mentor questions.	
Week 22	V is for Victories W is for Work Discuss the articles and ask the mentor questions.	
Week 23	X is for X-Cultural Competencies Y is for Your Network Discuss the articles and ask the mentor questions.	
Week 25	Z is for Zealous Discuss the article and ask the mentor questions. Self-Assessment for A to Z	Read and review Post- Release Checklist for Integration.

Week	Mentor Topics	Assignments for the Next Week
Week 26	Post-Release Checklist and Plan for Integration Discuss the Post-Release Checklist for Integration. Schedule and complete a warm handoff to the church mentor in your hometown. Make plans for weekly check-ins post-release for three months.	Develop the ultimate plan. What city will you return to? How will you get there? What family support do you have? What church home will provide support? Where will you live? What environment do you need to avoid so you don't return to prison? What programs do you need to access? What are you most concerned about?

KEY TRAITS AND SKILLS

A IS FOR ATTITUDE

> *Give thanks in all circumstances; for this God's will for you in Christ Jesus.*
> —1 Thessalonians 5:18

The only difference between a good day and a bad day is your attitude.

On any given day, life can be challenging for anyone. Our attitude reflects who we are. How important do you think having a positive attitude is? What is your mood each day when you get up or start your day, or about to go to bed? What about throughout the day? Do people like to be around you? Do you have a positive outlook, or do people avoid you? Do you bring others down? Are you hanging around inmates with negative attitudes that bring you down? Do you find yourself complaining about anything and everything? Do people make excuses for you, such as, "Well, that's just how he is"? Are you an energy drain in the unit? Do not be a Debbie Downer or a Ned Know-it-All.

Jon Gordon wrote an article called "How to Deal with Energy Vampires" after writing his book *The Energy Bus*. You do not want to be known as an "energy vampire" who sucks the air out of the room. You feel bored, overwhelmed, and frustrated by such people. These people exist. Make sure you are not one of them. Remember, bad attitudes are contagious, and so are good ones. How would people in your life describe your attitude?

According to the dictionary, the definition of *attitude* is "a way of thinking or feeling expressed through behaviors." Attitude can be expressed in various ways, such as job satisfaction, productivity, innovation, respect, helpfulness, and overall morale.

We all have blind spots, so the more you begin to uncover yours and take steps to improve, the more confident you will be, and more possibilities will arise. People rarely talk about blind spots. Think of it this way: You are driving a car, and you know you have a blind spot in your car. You drift in thought while driving one day and veer into the other lane. Depending on the conditions of the road and how quickly you act, the consequences can be dire. The same thing happens in your life. You cannot uncover your blind spots without help from people around you—so ask. Sometimes, the view we have of ourselves is not accurate.

Start each day with a gratitude journal or positive meditation or affirmations. Write out what you are grateful for, such as your family, friends, health, etc. Be specific. The more consistent you are with starting each day like this, the more your attitude will improve. Taking small steps each day creates an improved attitude. Once you find the beauty in the little things, your universe seems to expand in higher proportion.

Examine the language you use. Is it positive or negative? If it tends to be negative, start by rephrasing. Think before you say anything out loud. If you are feeling angry or frustrated, breathe before you speak. Surround yourself with positive people.

Don't you love being around positive people? Look for the good in people. Positive people inspire and motivate us. They make us smile. Do you make others smile?

Some people think it is cool to complain and speak negatively about everything.

Are you hanging out with people who have bad attitudes? How does it affect you and your attitude? What should you do to keep their lousy attitude from influencing you?

Do good work without expecting anything in return. Be willing to forgive. Learn from your mistakes, and do not beat yourself up mentally. When you make a mistake, get in the habit of thinking through what the experience has taught you, then move on. Do not dwell on negative things, people, or conversations. I believe part of my success is that I do not dwell on problems. I get into action and work toward a solution. My advice is to get into action, and a change in attitude will follow.

John C. Maxwell wrote a book titled *Attitude 101: What Every Leader Needs to Know*. This book is a practical guide and a great place to examine your thoughts, feelings, and behaviors at work. You can determine your circumstances by maintaining a positive attitude. You can take your first step toward leadership by improving your attitude at work, with family, and with friends. It starts with you.

Every moment is a chance to choose a positive attitude regardless of circumstances.

REFERENCES

Brown, Les, and Jim Rohn. n.d. *Why Attitude Is Everything*. https://www.youtube.com/watch?v=nbfFDnKkMvw.

Gordon, Jon. n.d. "How to Deal with an Energy Vampire." *Jon Gordon's Weekly Newsletter*. http://www.jongordon.com/positive-tip-energy-vampires.html.

Gordon, Jon. 2007. *The Energy Bus: 10 Rules to Fuel Your Life, Work, and Team with Positive Energy*. Hoboken, NJ: Wiley.

Maxwell, John. 2003. *Attitude 101: What Every Leader Needs to Know*. Nashville, TN: HarperCollins Leadership.

"The Attitude Test." n.d. https://www.3smartcubes.com/pages/tests/attitudetest/attitudetest_instructions/Online attitude assessments.

Attitude Self-Assessment Questions

In preparation for your weekly meeting with your mentor, answer the questions beforehand.

Questions	Responses
How self-aware are you?	
Have you ever taken an attitude test?	
Ask your family, friends, teachers, counselors, directors, and people around you about your attitude. What would they say? Interview five people you trust who will give you direct feedback about your attitude.	
What would your counselors, teachers, or prison staff members say about your attitude? If you do not know, ask.	
What would your family say about your attitude? If you do not know, ask.	
How do you handle a challenging situation when you hit a roadblock in life?	
Do you feel like you are adaptable? If yes, give an example.	
If you get off track or get stressed out, how do you get yourself back on track?	
In what area of keeping a positive attitude are you skilled?	
Based on the feedback you received from the five interviews, what is one area in which you could improve your attitude?	
What is one action step you can take to improve in this area?	
How will you know you are making progress?	

Attitude Mentor Questions

Questions to ask the mentee:	Write out the mentee's responses.
Describe your attitude from the self-assessment inventory.	
What did you learn from the attitude interviews you conducted about yourself? How many people, and who were they?	
Did any comments surprise you?	
What is one action step you can take to improve your attitude?	
How will you measure your improvement in this area?	
How can I support you?	
What went well during the mentoring session?	
Were there any challenges during the session?	
Assignment for next week:	

B IS FOR BEHAVIOR

> *Who among you is wise and understanding? Let him show by his good behavior his deeds in the gentleness of wisdom.*
>
> —James 3:13

When you embark on changing your behavior, you want to make sure you are clear about the behavior you want to change, according to Trudi Griffin (November 6, 2020). You must set clear goals. They need to be specific, measurable, and timely, and you must create a plan. Avoid making too many changes at a time. Think positively. Remind yourself of the benefits of making an effort. Stop blaming yourself. Every day is a new day. Think about the benefits of making the change. What is possible if you make the change? Choose behaviors *you* want to change! Ask yourself, "Is anyone else pressuring me to change or not change a behavior?"

One of the most effective approaches to behavioral change is taught by Dr. Marshall Goldsmith, the number one executive coach in the world. His approach works on changing behavior first and then perceptions of the people in our lives. We often think we show up one way in front of people, but people can see things we cannot see. These are called blind spots. With the help of a coach, they can be discovered positively and improve the direction of your life in all aspects.

As a certified Marshall Goldsmith coach, I have seen the power of the stakeholder-centered coaching approach with my clients. Stakeholders are the closest people to you that you interact with every day. Examples include your manager at work, employees, peers, and significant others. However, the first rule in coaching is that the client (that's you) must sincerely try to change and be open to coaching.

Dr. Goldsmith works with world-leading CEOs, and he says one reason they are so effective in leading people is they are always looking for ways to improve themselves. They are never satisfied with the way it is now. So, what is behavioral-based coaching? This type of coaching is focused on changing behavior.

Once you decide on an area you want to improve, it is essential to involve key stakeholders. This approach also focuses on the future or the past. Participants create a list of key stakeholders as part of the coaching process. Stakeholders are people you admire or will give honest feedback, such as teachers, clergy, counselors, warden, parole officers, or trusted family members.

If you are reading this book, it is most probable that you are still incarcerated. How could you get a jump start in using this approach now? First, with your mentor, identify a behavior from the character-strengths writing exercise you completed and want to continue to work on while in prison.

o To improve taking responsibility for all your actions
o To be grateful for everything in your life
o To tell the truth and be honest in all interactions
o To forgive yourself and others
o To control your emotions and responses to situations
o To believe and appreciate your uniqueness and potential
o To have the faith that your Creator has a purpose for your life

Make a list of people you interact with regularly. The list might include the unit prison staff members, housing mates, fellow inmates in classes you are taking, teachers, ministers, family members, etc. The ideal list would include yourself and five to seven other people. These people can help you on your journey, should be helpful and supportive, and willing to put the past in the past. We will call them *stakeholders*.

A simplified version of this process is to ask each stakeholder if they would be willing to be your developmental partner, be honest with you, provide actionable suggestions once a month, and be someone you can work with for at least six months. You must have the discipline to check in with each stakeholder monthly. Remind them what you are working on. Ask each person if you are making progress, if they see no change, or if you are going backward. Based on your behavior last month, ask what ideas or actionable suggestions they might have for you to try next month. Say, "Thank you" (this is not a debate). You do not argue with your stakeholders. You asked for their feedback, so accept it.

Based on the initial feedback, you develop an action plan with the help of your mentor for this unit.

Behavior Action Plan

Behavior	Suggestions	People	Education
What is the behavior you will focus on for the next six months?	This is where you place the suggestions from each stakeholder.	Check in with your stakeholders once a month. Check in with your mentor each week. Use daily questions each day and rate your progress (see next page for an example).	A mentor-provided resource to help your progress, such as a book, magazine article, etc.

Behavior Choices

Choose one from the previous page listed.

Another effective tool Marshall Goldsmith personally subscribes to and suggests for all clients is daily questions. Dr. Goldsmith uses this practice himself and has for over twenty years. It is a way to present his work, build accountability, and build muscle memory.

I have seen firsthand that the exercise initially seems a bit uncomfortable. After a few months, what happens is you internalize the questions. They become part of your daily thoughts. As this happens, behavior changes begin to happen naturally. This tool is a great way to track your progress. Here is an example of questions you can create for yourself. These questions should support what is important to you. Daily questions are a way to build muscle memory and keep what you are working on visible so it does not disappear.

Instructions:

- Use daily questions for the next six months.
- Ask yourself each question.
- Rate your daily progress for each question (1 = poor and 5 = average, and 10 = excellent).

Daily Questions are a habit building tool. This practice is your accountability partner to change your behavior. See example below.

Sample Questions (can be modified to fit the behavior you are working on—write out 5 to 6 questions that fit you)	Monday	Tuesday	Wednesday	Thursday	Friday	Saturday	Sunday
Are you doing your best to take responsibility for your actions?	8						
Did you do your best to be aware of your emotions and control your response?	7						
Are you doing your best to focus on your purpose?	9						
Are you doing your best to set daily goals and make progress on them?	10						

Are you doing your best to believe in your self-worth and that you are unique?	7						

Now create your template based on the behavior you are working on. (Create questions that will help reinforce the behavior daily.)

Sample Questions (can be modified to fit the behavior you are working on—write out 5 to 6 questions that fit you)	Monday	Tuesday	Wednesday	Thursday	Friday	Saturday	Sunday
Are you doing your best to…							
Are you doing your best to…							
Are you doing your best to …							
Are you doing your best to …							
Are you doing your best to …							

Use daily questions for the next six months.

Ask yourself each question daily.

Rate your daily progress for each question (1 = poor and 5 = average, and 10 = excellent).

While there is no shortage of behaviors to work on, we can all change. Start with one that will truly impact the future of your life. We know it is possible.

REFERENCES

Goldsmith, Marshall. 2020. "Stakeholder-Centered Coaching."
    https://www.marshallgoldsmith.com.
Griffin, T. 2020. "How to Change Behavior" (November 6, 2020).
    https://www.wikihow.comChange-Behavior.

Behavior Self-Assessment Questions

Questions	Responses
Are you coachable? What is the reason you are coachable or not coachable?	
Do you have the courage, humility, and discipline to take this on?	
What is one behavior you would like to focus on improving?	
What is one thing you can start to do differently now?	
What is one thing you should start doing?	
What is one thing to stop doing?	
What is one thing to continue doing?	
What is possible for your life if you can make this change?	
What could stop you from making this change?	
What has not making this change cost you?	
What stakeholders would you list to get feedback?	
What are one or two questions you could add or change to the daily questions to help reinforce the behavior change you want to make?	

Behavior Mentor Assessment Questions

Questions to ask the mentee:	Write out the mentee's responses.
Are you coachable? What is the reason you are coachable or not coachable?	
Do you have the courage, humility, and discipline to take this on?	
What is one behavior you would like to focus on improving?	
What is one thing you can start to do differently starting now?	
What is one thing you should start doing?	
What is one thing you should stop doing?	
What is one thing you should continue doing?	
What is possible for your life if you can make this change?	
What could stop you from making this change?	
What has not making this change cost you?	
What one or two questions could you add to the daily questions to help reinforce the behavior change you want to make?	
How are the daily behavior questions going?	
Assignment for next week:	

C IS FOR COMMUNICATION

> *Let everything you say be good and helpful, so that your words will be an encouragement to those that hear them.*
> —Ephesians 4:29

When men and women are released from prison, they face unique communication challenges as they reintegrate into society. Here are some aspects that all genders may need to adjust. These include social skills, stigma, building trust, emotional expression, adapting to technology, language, actively listening, conflict resolution, and nonverbal behaviors.

- Social skills and norms: After spending an extended period in prison, individuals may struggle to adapt to social norms and expectations outside of the correctional system. They may need support understanding appropriate communication styles, body language, and overall social interactions.
- Stigma and discrimination: Both men and women may face stigmatization and discrimination because of their past incarceration. This can affect their ability to communicate effectively and build healthy relationships with peers, colleagues, and potential employers.
- Building trust: Individuals reentering society from prison often face skepticism and mistrust from others. They may experience challenges in establishing trust and being perceived as credible communicators.
- Emotional expression: Incarceration can lead to emotional suppression and limited outlets for expression. Men may find it challenging to open up and communicate their emotions after being conditioned to hide vulnerability. Encouraging emotional expression and providing a safe space for communication can be crucial.
- Adapting to technology: Advancements in technology during their time in prison may have left individuals unfamiliar with current communication tools and platforms. Helping them understand and navigate technology can be necessary for effective communication in various areas of life, including job searches and staying connected with support networks.
- Language and slang: Prison slang and jargon may differ significantly from everyday language. Individuals may need help adjusting their communication style to match societal language norms, particularly in professional settings.

- Active listening and empathy: Effective communication involves active listening and empathy. Spending significant time in an environment where these skills were not consistently valued or practiced can make it challenging to engage in meaningful conversations. Encouraging and teaching these skills can enhance their ability to connect with others.
- Conflict resolution: Conflict resolution strategies learned in prison, such as aggression or avoidance, may not be effective or accepted outside of that environment. Guiding healthy conflict resolution techniques can help individuals navigate conflicts constructively.
- Non-verbal communication: The subtleties of non-verbal communication, such as body language and facial expressions, may have been altered during incarceration. Helping individuals relearn and interpret non-verbal cues can be necessary for successful communication. One example is eye contact. In prison, it was not safe to look someone in the eyes. Outside of prison, avoiding eye contact could create a lack of trust. There is much to unlearn and relearn.

Ex-offenders must learn to communicate effectively to transition back into society successfully. The importance of this is magnified because of issues that may prevent an ex-offender's adjustment to society, such as lower literacy rates, emotional and mental issues, anger that affects communication, and negative perceptions of society at large (Contreras, R. A., June 2018, CSUSB Scholarworks).

Certain offenders can adjust after their release and live productive lives if they learn how to communicate effectively.

Here are some communication tips:

- Be honest.
- Show respect.
- Talk in simple language.
- Remember how you dress communicates.
- Do not mislead.
- Be yourself.

For a mentor, it is essential to approach these challenges with sensitivity, recognizing the unique experiences and needs of everyone. Tailoring support and communication to address these specific challenges can significantly enhance their successful reintegration into society.

Poor communication skills create problems for you. You have read "A Is for Attitude," "B Is for Behaviors," and "C Is for Communication." How would you assess yourself? Where are your opportunities for self-improvement? You have taken the first three steps to become more aware of who you are and can become. Let's keep going.

REFERENCES

"Communication Skills: How to Improve Communication Skills, 7 Tips." https://www.youtube.com/watch?v=mPRUNGGORDo.

Dale Carnegie. https://www.dalecarnegie.com/en/topics/people-skills.

"Improve your Listening Skills with Active Listening" by Mindtools.com.

https://www.youtube.com/watch?v=t2z9mdX1j4A.

Mehrabian, Albert. "Communication Model," in "7 38 55 rule of Communication," by P. Mulder. https://www.toolshero.com/communication-skills/communication-model-mehrabian/.

Communication Self-Assessment Questions

Questions	Responses
Rate your communication skills on a scale of 1–10, with 1 being poor and 10 being excellent: _____Active listening _____Speaking _____Writing _____Social skills _____Discrimination concerns _____Nonverbal communication _____Body language _____Tone of voice _____Ability to build trust _____Emotional awareness _____Ability to adapt to technology such as computers, cell phones, and texting _____Ability to deal with conflict constructively	
What is an area you need to start working on first?	
In what area could you improve your communication skills in prison? In what area could your communication skills improve at home or work?	
What outside resources will help you improve in this area?	
Have you ever participated in Toastmasters, Dale Carnegie, read communication books, watched YouTube videos on the subject, or used communication apps or personal-development courses to improve your communication?	

Communication Mentor Questions

Questions to ask the mentee:	Write out the mentee's responses.
Describe your communication skill strengths.	
Describe your communication skill weaknesses. What are your plans to improve in these areas?	
How important do you think effective communication skills are for life?	
Have you ever participated in Toastmasters, Dale Carnegie, read communication books, watched YouTube videos on the subject, or used communication apps or personal-development courses to improve your communication?	
Are you open to participating in one of the above activities to improve?	
What is one action step you can take to improve in this area?	
How will you know you are making progress?	
Assignment for next week:	
How are the daily behavior questions going?	

> *Am I being people-pressured or spirit-led?*
> —Galatians 1:10

We often make decisions based on our experiences. Sometimes they turn out, and sometimes they do not. Some decisions are trivial, and some are life changing. Whatever you decide can change the direction of your life. If you regret certain decisions, what can you learn from them going forward?

According to Tasha Rube (2020, 1), decision-making is a two-step process. The first step is to frame the decision, and the second is to make the decision. Step one, framing the decision, includes outlining the issue and dealing with your emotions. Making decisions when you are emotional is never a good idea. Approach the situation with a rational mind and objectivity. Do not overload yourself with information. Prioritize what you know.

Some people overanalyze situations, which often leads to analysis paralysis. Instead, use the 80/20 rule. You can probably proceed if you have 80 percent of the information you need. Sometimes delaying a decision for additional information can create new problems. Consider multiple options. List everything you can think of. Consider the pros and cons. Consider the risks and rewards.

Step two is to make the decision. Realize you have your own internal biases. View the issue from different perspectives. Seek advice. Just because you decide on an easy solution, realize it may not be the best.

Create an action plan. Write out the steps.

Commit to your decision; do not second-guess yourself. Once you make the decision and move forward, evaluate the decision. Finally, have a backup plan. Consider things that might not go the way you intended.

Now let us put this into practice this week. What decision do you need to make?

REFERENCES

Rube, T. 2020. "How to Make Better Decisions" (November 12). https://www.wikihow.com/Mke-Better-Decisions

Decision-Making Self-Assessment Questions

Questions	Responses
What is a decision you need to make?	
What is your motivation for making the decision? Understanding your motivation can keep you from making a bad decision. Outline the issue.	
If you had to decide right now, could you do so objectively, or do you feel your emotions will get in the way?	
Take a breath and write out all the options you have. Consider the pros and cons. What are they?	
Are you open to participating in one of the above activities to improve?	
Pretend you are advising a friend or family member. What advice would you give them if they were making this decision themselves? (Sometimes, we are better at advising others than taking our advice.)	
What are the risks and rewards of making this decision?	
What biases do you bring to making this decision?	
Create an action plan.	
What did you decide?	
After the fact, evaluate the decision. Were you happy with the outcome? What could you have done better? What can you learn from this?	

Decision-Making Mentor Questions

Questions to ask the mentee:	Write out the mentee's responses.
What is a decision you need to make?	
What is your motivation for making the decision? Understanding your motivation can keep you from making bad decisions. Outline the issue.	
If you had to decide right now, could you do so objectively, or do you feel your emotions will get in the way?	
Take a breath and write out all the options you have. Consider the process and cons. What are they?	
Are you open to participating in one of the above activities to improve?	
Pretend you are advising a friend or family member. What advice would you give them if they were making this decision themselves? (Sometimes, we are better at advising others than taking our advice.)	
What are the risks and rewards of making this decision?	
What biases do you bring to making this decision?	
Create an action plan.	
What did you decide?	
After the fact, evaluate the division. Were you happy with the outcome? What could you have done better? What can you learn from this?	

Questions to ask the mentee:	Write out the mentee's responses.
Assignment for next week:	
How are the daily behavior questions going?	

> *Change is never painful. Only the resistance to change is.*
> *—The Buddha*

Emotional intelligence is "the capacity to beware of, control and express one's emotions and to handle interpersonal relationships with empathy" (*Oxford Languages Dictionary*). The actual state you want to achieve is equanimity. Equanimity is defined as mental calmness and composure, and evenness of temper.

We all experience emotions. What we do with those emotions differentiates us from others. You might know IQ (intelligence quotient) is important, but EQ (emotional intelligence; emotional quotient) is even more critical. Mike Robbins (2018), the author of *Bring Your Whole Self to Work*, shared that Jeff, the keynote speaker and talent manager at Adobe, said, "Your IQ might get you in the door, but EQ is what will get you promoted." Daniel Goleman noted that a leader's success is two-thirds emotional intelligence and one-third IQ. So, what does that mean to you in your life?

When our emotions are not under control, we take actions we might not usually take. Emotions are feelings that result in physical and psychological changes that influence thoughts and behaviors. What is emotional intelligence? It is the ability to be intelligent with our emotions. It is the capacity to be aware of, control, and express one's emotions and handle relationships well. Emotional intelligence is a combination of personal competence and social competence. Under personal competence, there is self-awareness and self-management. Under social competence, there is social awareness and relationship management.

- Self-awareness is recognizing and understanding your emotions as they happen and appreciating your general tendencies for responding to and defending people and situations.
- Self-management is using awareness of your emotions to choose what you say and do to direct your behavior and manage your reactions positively.
- Social awareness is understanding where the other person is coming from, whether you agree.
- Relationship management is using awareness of the other person's emotions to choose what you say and do to direct your behavior positively.

Emotional intelligence takes time to develop. It is a skill that needs to be developed and practiced. Think about a person whose emotional intelligence you admire. See what you can learn from them. Also, to become more self-aware, take a free online emotional intelligence assessment or read Daniel Goleman's book *Emotional Intelligence*.

Emotional intelligence and equanimity can play a significant role in helping an ex-offender successfully transition back into society. Here are some ways:

What is emotional intelligence ,and how can you develop it? Emotional intelligence involves the ability to recognize, understand, and manage our emotions and the emotions of others. Ex-offenders who have developed emotional intelligence skills are better equipped to handle different situations that may arise during their re-entry process. They can handle stress, maintain good relationships with others, and make sound decisions. *Emotional Intelligence 2.0* and *The EQ Difference* are two great books to support your growth.

How can you build empathy? Empathy is an important component of emotional intelligence. It enables ex-offenders to understand the feelings and emotions of others, particularly the families and loved ones who are also affected by their transition. This helps build better, meaningful relationships with others and offers a sense of belonging.

How can you further develop resilience? Successful re-entry into society requires resilience, which is the ability to recover from setbacks and bounce back from difficulties. Think back to things you have already overcome. How did you do that? You have some proven strategies already. Who was your support group? What judgments did you make? What solutions did you come up with? Ex-offenders need to be strong psychologically to overcome the challenges they may face during the transition. Equanimity helps develop resilience by enabling ex-offenders to remain calm and composed even in challenging situations.

How can you manage your anger and frustrations? Managing anger and frustration is an important aspect of emotional intelligence. Ex-offenders who have learned to manage their anger and frustrations are more likely to avoid conflict and better regulate their behavior. By understanding their triggers and practicing emotional regulation techniques, they can better control their emotions and communicate more effectively. What programs are available in the prison to learn how to deal with now?

What are the benefits to you in becoming more emotionally intelligent? You can improve your relationships, feel more confident, become more self-aware, be less impulsive, possess the ability to be happier more often, and have developed social skills (Nalin 2017, 4). Thinking back over your life, when did your emotions get in the way of doing the right thing? Or when have you made decisions based on your emotions instead of being objective, and what was the result?

In summary, emotional intelligence and equanimity can help ex-offenders develop a range of essential emotional skills for a successful re-entry into society. These skills enable them to build better relationships, manage stress, and make better decisions.

REFERENCES

"Emotional Intelligence Test." The Global Leadership Foundation. https://globalleadershipfoundation.com/geit/eitest.html

"Emotional Intelligence." YouTube video by The Life School.
   https://www.youtube.com/watch?v=LgUCyWhJf6s.
"Emotional Intelligence." YouTube video with Daniel Goleman.
   https://www.youtube.com/watch?v=Y7m9eNoB3NU.

Emotional Intelligence Self-Assessment Questions

Questions	Responses
Take the EI online assessment. What did you learn about yourself after you took the EI assessment?	
How do you feel today? What is the reason you feel this way?	
How do you think emotional intelligence will impact your life?	
Describe how you see yourself. Include your strengths, weaknesses, emotions, and motivation. Do you have an overall positive or negative impression of yourself?	
Write out your first name and last name. Using the letters of your name, create words that express your positive traits.	
Write about a time when you let your emotions take over. How did your reactions make you feel afterward?	
What triggers create stress for you? Do you know when stress is coming on? Do you know how to manage stress?	
What are your expectations for your life and work relationships?	

Emotional Intelligence Mentor Questions

Questions to ask the mentee:	Write out the mentee's responses.
What did you learn about yourself after you took the EI assessment?	
Complete the following: I am most happy when… I feel embarrassed when… I think negative thoughts about myself when…	
How do you think emotional intelligence will impact your life?	
Describe how you see yourself. Include your strengths, weaknesses, emotions, and motivation. Do you have an overall positive or negative impression of yourself?	
Tell me about a time when you let your emotions take over. How did your reactions make you feel afterward?	
What causes you to lose your cool? How do you manage your anger?	
What triggers create stress for you? Do you know when stress is coming on? Do you know how to manage stress?	
How long does it take for you to get frustrated or angry?	
What are your expectations for your life and work relationships?	
Assignment for next week:	
How are the daily questions going?	

F IS FOR FINANCE

Prayer

> *Father God, we lift before you those who are struggling with finances. We ask that you provide jobs to those who need them and continue to bless your children so they can continue to be a blessing to others. In Jesus's name, amen.*

What is the importance of creating a budget? You are probably not a financial expert, as it is not generally taught in schools. The exception to this assumption is if you were working in the finance world before incarceration, which is why you are in prison. Regardless, your life has changed dramatically. How financially literate are you? This is where your mentor can help you prepare pre- and post-release plans for the reality of the situation.

Some people avoid looking at budgeting, which is always a mistake. We need to develop good financial habits, and it is never too late. Intelligent financial strategies have nothing to do with gender, age, ethnicity, or marital status. Knowing is not enough. We all need to practice and develop good daily habits. I may know a lot about dieting or eating healthy, but it makes no difference if I do not apply what I know. It is the same with financial literacy. We must build that financial muscle.

Common financial mistakes are made when you do not prepare, overspend, don't create a budget, use a credit card without having the money, use some type of payday lender with exorbitant interest rates, do not understand the difference between needs and wants, do not do your homework when it comes to making purchases, and make decisions based on emotions.

Managing where your money goes, regardless of income, is key. A simple example is when you say to yourself, "I want a large soft drink from a fast-food place every day. I do not need it." Let's say it costs $2. ($2 a day × 365 days = $730) What could you do with $730 instead? Or you want a pack of cigarettes. The average price of a pack is $7. (365 days × $7 =$2,555) What could you do with $2,555 extra in a year if you did not stop for cigarettes? Maybe you could start a savings account. Little things add up, so you must be careful.

Keep records of all your receipts and what you spend to see where the money goes when you are released.

Let's start by creating two budgets upon release from prison, where you will be given $100.

How do you plan on using it?

Immediate Expenses	Amount	Option(s), each with a different cost
Transportation		Ex: Bus; friend, other, walk, etc.
Food		
Housing		Halfway house, shelter, friend's house, other
Total	$100	

Now let us budget for three months after release. Suppose you have a job and make $2,000 a month.

Expenses	Amount	Option(s)	Changes
Housing		Living with family, a roommate, or by yourself (each has a different cost associated with it)	
Transportation		Walking/biking; public transportation; car/insurance	
Food		Groceries and household expenses; eating one meal out a week	
Personal items		Basic needs; clothes	
Phone		Cellphone/plan	
Debt		No debt; childcare; child support; legal fees; credit card	
Entertainment		None; Netflix; go to the movies	
Total monthly expenses			

The total must not exceed what you earn monthly. Remember, taxes will be taken from your paycheck, so calculate your actual take-home pay. What things can you do without?

Finance Self-Assessment Questions

Questions	Responses
How financially literate are you?	
What did you learn from completing the first budget activity with $100?	
What did you learn from creating a three-month budget?	
What are your financial goals?	
What financial mistakes have you made in the past? How can you correct them moving forward?	
What purchases have you made in the past that were impulsive?	
How will you earn a living?	
How can you earn extra income legally?	
Realistically, how much money do you have to make each month to live?	
Do you know your credit score?	
What happens if there is an emergency?	
Did you have credit cards before? How responsible were you with credit cards?	
What is one step you can take toward increasing your financial literacy?	

Finance Mentor Questions

As the mentor, prepare in advance additional resources/questions based on your experience.

Questions to ask the mentee:	Write out the mentee's responses.
How financially literate are you?	
What did you learn from completing the first budget activity with $100?	
What did you learn from creating a three-month budget?	
What are your financial goals?	
What financial mistakes have you made in the past? How can you correct them moving forward?	
What purchases have you made in the past that were impulsive?	
How will you earn a living?	
How can you earn extra income legally?	
Realistically, how much money do you have to make each month to live?	
Do you know your credit score?	

Questions to ask the mentee:	Write out the mentee's responses.
What happens if there is an emergency?	
Did you have credit cards before? How responsible were you with credit cards?	
What is one step you can take toward increasing your financial literacy?	
What do you want to learn from me on this topic?	
Assignment for next week:	
How are the daily behavior questions going?	

G IS FOR GOAL SETTING

> *In their hearts, humans plan their course, and the Lord establishes their steps.*
> —Proverbs 16:9

According to *Inc. Magazine*, you are 42 percent more likely to achieve your goals if you write them down. Writing down your goals forces you to get clear about exactly what you want and can motivate you to complete them. Wake up to your goals, visualize them, and review them daily. If you can picture them, you are more likely to achieve your goals.

First, visualize what you want to accomplish in the next year and then write it down. What do you want for your career, finances, spirituality, health and well-being, family, friends, hobbies, etc.? Maybe the first thing is to write down what type of job you want when you are released from prison. What are your top three priorities when you are released?

Let's get started. Set up short-term and long-term goals. Short-term goals are something you want to do very soon. An example could be writing a résumé or taking a new class.

Long-term goals require time and planning. Create a picture of where you want to be one year from now, three years, or five years from now. Work backward and write out how you can achieve these goals. What do you have to do month by month to make progress toward the end goal? Review your progress monthly. Prioritize your goals and immediately start one thing. Once you begin to write your goals, make sure they are SMART goals.

SMART is an acronym.

S	Specific
M	Measurable
A	Achievable
R	Realistic
T	Time-bound

S is for *specific*. Make sure your goals are detailed and clear. *M* is for *measurable*, which means you know when you have completed the goal. *A* is for *achievable*, which includes how you will do it. *R* is for *realistic*, which means achieving it in the time frame you designated is possible. *T* is *time-bound*, which means there is a set time frame for when you will have the goal done.

Let's test your understanding.

Which one of these is a SMART goal:

a. I want to go home.
b. I want to earn a degree.
c. I will save for retirement.
d. I will ask my supervisor for two weeks of vacation beginning July 12.

The answer is *d*. Explain.

Which one of these is a SMART goal:

a. I want to lose ten pounds.
b. I want to be healthy.
c. I will walk thirty minutes a day to lose a pound a week because I want to lose ten pounds in two and a half months.
d. I want to drink more water.

The answer is *c*. Explain.

REFERENCES

Economy, P. 2020. "This Is the Way to Write Down Your Goals for Faster Success" (February 24). https://www.inc.com/peter-economy/this-is-way-you-need-to-write-down-your-goals-for-faster-success.html#:~:text=The%20results%3F-,You%20are%2042%20percent%20more%20likely%20to%20achieve%20your%20goals,tasks%20necessary%20for%20your%20success.

Goal-Setting Self-Assessment Questions

Questions	Responses
What is important to you right now?	
What sort of work do you like?	
What sort of work don't you like?	
What are three short-term goals you have?	
What are three long-term goals?	
Write out your short-term goals.	
Using the SMART goal method, write your three long-term goals.	
What is your plan for reviewing both short-term and long-term goals?	
How will you know you have been successful?	
How will you know when to be flexible about goal setting?	

Goal-Setting Mentor Questions

Questions to ask the mentee:	Write out the mentee's responses.
What is important to you right now?	
What sort of work do you like?	
What sort of work don't you like?	
Where do you see yourself living post-release?	
What are three short-term goals you have?	
What are three long-term goals?	
Share with me your written short-term goals.	
Share with me your long-term SMART goals.	
What is your plan for reviewing both short-term and long-term goals? How often? How will you know when you have been successful?	
How do you know when it is essential to be flexible? (Change your focus on goals as your life changes.)	
Assignment for next week:	
How are the daily behavior questions going?	

> *Health is the greatest gift, contentment the greatest*
> *wealth, faithfulness the best relationship.*
> —Gautama Buddha

How do you create and live a vibrant and healthy lifestyle regardless of your circumstances? A healthy lifestyle is much more than eating healthy foods and maintaining a good weight. It involves every part of your life, from managing stress, drinking enough water, sleep, exercise, not smoking, not doing drugs, and not drinking too much. A healthy lifestyle can mean reducing screen time and reading or walking instead. It can mean getting up and doing your assigned chores. This will be true when you are released, so it is better to practice now to be ready post-release.

In addition to physical health, there is also mental health. According to the National Institute of Mental Health (NIMH), in the United States, approximately one in five adults (about 51.5 million individuals) experiences mental illness yearly. Mental illness encompasses many conditions, including depression, anxiety disorders, bipolar disorder, schizophrenia, eating disorders, and substance abuse disorders, among others.

There are many ways you can stay healthy and well after your release from prison. Here are a few suggestions:

- Develop a healthy routine: Establish a routine that includes regular exercise, healthy eating, getting enough sleep, and avoiding drugs and alcohol.
- Practice stress management: Take steps to manage stress and anxiety, such as deep breathing exercises, meditation, yoga, or talking to a therapist or counselor.
- Stay connected: Establish and maintain positive relationships with family and friends and participate in social and community activities.
- Maintain a positive outlook: Focus on the present moment and try not to dwell on negative feelings or events from the past. Look for opportunities to learn and grow and embrace a positive attitude.
- Reach out and help someone else. This can be very healing.
- Continue learning: Pursue education or training opportunities or explore new hobbies and interests that support your health and well-being.
- Seek support: Reach out to support groups for ex-offenders or consider counseling or therapy if you struggle with mental health or addiction issues. If you have been

diagnosed with a mental health issue, taking and staying on your medication is vital to stay mentally well.

Most people try to take on too much and fail. Making small and gradual changes will pay off in the long run.

When you look at the list, you can see how hard all those things in your current world are, so setting goals and having a plan is the first step. Your mentor can support you; the daily questions can serve as your accountability partner.

REFERENCES

Waehner, P. 2020. "How to Live a Healthier Lifestyle" (July 27). https://www.verywellfir.com/simple-ways-to-live-a-healthy-lifestyle.

Health Self-Assessment Questions

Questions	Responses
Make a list of your unhealthy lifestyle choices.	
Make a list of your healthy lifestyle choices.	
How can you maintain a healthy lifestyle in prison? What is one small change you can make?	
Do you believe this is possible?	
Is it something you are willing to do?	
What are the benefits of making this change?	
What will it cost you if you do not make this change?	
When you are released, there will be new temptations. How will you manage these?	

Health Mentor Questions

Questions to ask the mentee:	Write out the mentee's responses.
Share with me your list of unhealthy lifestyle choices.	
Share with me your list of healthy lifestyle choices.	
How can you maintain a healthy lifestyle in prison? What is one small change you can make?	
Do you believe this is possible?	
Is it something you are willing to do?	
What are the benefits of making this change?	
What will it cost you if you do not make this change?	
When you are released, there will be new temptations. How will you manage these?	
Assignment for next week:	
How are the daily behavior questions going?	

> *The integrity of the upright guides them, but the*
> *unfaithful are destroyed by their duplicity.*
> —Proverbs 11:3

This is not a make-wrong word. It is doing what you say all the time regardless of whether anyone is watching you or knows. It is the integrity of self. You are keeping and honoring your word. It is a state of being. It is keeping your promises to yourself, your friends, and your family. You will be amazed at how free you feel when you know you can keep your word to yourself and others, and they can count on you. (It does not mean always saying yes.)

Here is a situation to consider: Are you great at work about keeping your word, but when it comes to yourself, not so much—or vice versa? Take an honest look at your life and decide where you can improve your integrity muscle. It will take practice, but each day you try, you grow. To make this trait real, you need to dig deep and speak truthfully to yourself.

Here are some areas to think about: Do you gossip about others? Have you taken things without paying for them? Have you taken office supplies home for personal use? Have you used the school or company copier for copying personal items? Do you tell little white lies and justify it? Do you exceed the speed limit? Have you ever parked in a handicapped-accessible parking space even though you are not handicapped? Do you think the rules do not apply to you? Have you hurt someone's feelings and never apologized? Have you been charged less for an item at a store and failed to tell them they charged you the wrong amount? Have you ever found money on the floor at a store and failed to turn it in? Have you disclosed confidential information about your family or a project? Have you used school or work time to be on social media when you were supposed to be working? Have you ever made a mistake at work and failed to own it? Did you fail to meet a company deadline? Do you follow company policies 100 percent of the time? Have you taken credit for someone else's work? Have you committed a crime and not been honest about it? Or do you continue to lie to yourself? Have you ever compromised your values? Do you have the courage to tell the truth?

Or maybe you are great at keeping your word with others but not as much when it comes to yourself. Do you have integrity for yourself? Do you keep your word to yourself? Do you tell yourself you will change and then not follow through? You matter. Now is the best time to become the best version of you.

Look to improve in this area every day. How can you build your integrity muscle?

Be honest. When you make a mistake, own it. Be a person of your word. Become someone everyone can count on, no matter what. Know that you can rely on yourself. Know that you are your word. The more you flex the integrity muscle, the stronger you become. It is just like working out. You know you have arrived when you can count on your word and yourself. Integrity is a crucial characteristic of leadership.

Good luck getting stronger every day.

Integrity Self-Assessment Questions

Questions	Responses
What does integrity mean to you?	
Is integrity important in life? Explain.	
When you read the examples, did you see yourself in any of them?	
Who do you admire because of their integrity? What company displays integrity?	
What examples are you aware of in business when the leader failed to have integrity? What happened? If you're not aware of any examples, research and share.	
What is one area that you can work on for yourself?	
How do you justify your behavior when your integrity is not intact?	
How will you know you are making progress?	
How will you know when you can keep your word? To yourself? To others?	

Integrity Mentor Questions

As the mentor, what additional resources can you share with your mentee?

Questions to ask the mentee:	Write out the mentee's responses.
What does integrity mean to you?	
What did you think of some of the examples provided? Let's discuss a few things.	
Have you ever looked at integrity in this way? What surprised you?	
If you were in a leadership position, how would you model integrity?	
How do you currently demonstrate integrity?	
What happens when a leader does not model integrity? What happened to the organization? To the culture? To the people? Can you give some specific examples?	
How will you measure your improvement in this area?	
How can I support you?	
Assignment for next week:	
How are the daily behavior questions going?	

> *Jesus answered, "I am the way and the truth and the life. No one comes to the Father except through me."*
> —John 14:6

Regardless of how long you have been incarcerated, I pray you have taken advantage of a faith-based ministry program while in prison and maintained a daily spiritual practice. I have had the opportunity to talk with men and women who have participated in the Kairos ministry and Bridges for Life. Most of the men I have spoken with did not join Kairos ministry when first introduced to the program. Some of their reasons for resisting were that they were already affiliated with a gang—what more did they need? For some, they thought it was losing control. Some just got tired of denying they needed something more and took advantage of the program. For the men I have spoken with who have gone through the Kairos ministry program, they all said it was life changing. They had no idea what was possible. For the women I have spoken with who participated in the Bridges to Life program, they said when they went into the program, they thought they had forgiven themselves for the situation that led them to prison. Once in the program, they found out they had a lot more work to do on themselves and with the families of their victims. Once they completed the program, they felt a new sense of freedom they had never experienced.

Accepting Christ into your life is life changing. As resilient as I am, I could not have become the person I am without having Christ at the center of my life.

How do you keep Christ at the center of your life? For me, I start and end each day in prayer. It helps ground me. I also include three to five things I am grateful for. At first, it may not seem like you have much to be thankful for, but the more you look, the more you will see what you have.

According to Kathy and Neal Pollard (*Christian Living*, 2013), there are twenty-five ways to keep Christ in the center of your life. I could not have said it better myself, so I am quoting him:

1. I will absorb myself in the practice of prayer.
2. I will actively practice kindness.
3. I will find someone each day with whom to share Him.
4. I will watch what I allow to grow in my heart.
5. I will carefully consider how what I do affects my influence.

6. I will actively encourage the people I encounter daily.
7. I will assume and look for the best in others.
8. I will nurture a hatred of sin and love of sinners.
9. I will treat Scripture as a daily nourishment for my soul.
10. I will keep a spiritual song in my heart.
11. I will reflect meaningfully on the price He paid at Calvary.
12. I will guard my tongue.
13. I will think lovingly about heaven.
14. I will contemplate ways to be in the church's work.
15. I will love His church with a passion
16. I will cut out the tendency to rationalize or defend wrongdoing.
17. I will be discerning about what is spiritual or defense wrongdoings.
18. I will grow in my understanding of what true love is.
19. I will humbly acknowledge the greatness and power of God.
20. I will do everything in my power to help answer His prayer for unity.
21. I will pursue souls with the same vigor He did.
22. I will look for ways to turn the conversation into a spiritual one.
23. I will long for times of worship and devotion.
24. I will care less and less about my rights, feelings, and desires.
25. I will think, speak, act, and look more like Him every day.

REFERENCES

Pollard, K, and N. Pollard. 2013. "25 ways to keep Christ at the center of your life" (November 17). https://life-and-favor.com/2013/03/11/25-ways-to-keep-christ-at-the-center-of-my-life/.

Jesus Self-Assessment Questions

Questions	Responses
What faith-based programs have you participated in? If you have, what programs? If not, what is your rationale?	
What impact have they made in your life? What have you learned?	
How have your feelings changed?	
What did you think of the article and list of twenty-five ways to keep Christ at the center of your life?	
How do you plan to use the list?	
What can you commit to practicing in your life?	

Jesus Mentor Questions

Questions to ask the mentee:	Write out the mentee's responses.
What faith-based programs have you participated in? If you have, what programs? If not, what is your rationale?	
What impact have they made in your life? What have you learned?	
How have your feelings changed?	
What did you think of the article and list of twenty-five ways to keep Christ at the center of your life?	
How do you plan on using the list?	
What can you commit to practicing in your life?	
Assignment for next week:	
How are the daily behavior questions going?	

K IS FOR KNOWLEDGEABLE

> *Your work is to discover your world and then with all your heart give yourself to it.*
> —Gautama Buddha

How prepared are you for when you leave prison? What programs have you taken advantage of while being incarcerated? Did your prison offer GED-high school equivalency, high school diploma, community college, vocational school, certifications, life-skills training, or entrepreneurship programs? How can you become more knowledgeable than you are today? Do you have a plan?

What opportunities can you still take advantage of while in prison? What do you need to know? What skills or assessments do you need that you may be lacking? Are there certifications or education that would enhance your situation? How are you going to fund what is next? What do you need to research? To whom might you need to speak?

Decide what you want to learn. Do you want to go wide or deep? Do you want to specialize in an area? Develop a plan to gain the knowledge you need to fill the gaps.

Knowledge is defined as facts, information, and skills you learn through education and experience. How can you increase your knowledge? You can read. You can ask questions. You can seek a mentor to help. You can follow the checklists in this book. Is training available to enhance your skill set? Is there an organization you could join post-release?

What can you volunteer to learn? You can stretch yourself and take on new projects to learn and assist others. Keep an open mind. It takes time to learn new things. You will make mistakes but learn from them. Notice how you feel when you are learning new things. It may be uncomfortable as you are outside your comfort zone.

How can you begin to enhance your technology skills? The world outside of prison is changing so fast regarding technology. There is always more to learn, and it changes daily. Examples include computers, cell phones, Bluetooth in the car, ATMs, paying for things from your cell phone, and social applications, just to name a few. How aware are you of these changes?

Examine other areas in your life where you may need to learn. Do you participate in deliberate practice and set aside time to master new skills? What information is missing for you to increase your mastery? The only way to learn is to read, talk, practice, and demonstrate proficiency over time.

Now it is time to prepare your plan for post release. This week refer to the back of the book. Complete the following for next week: the application exercise, create a functional resume, get proof of education or certifications, and create a list of three people who could serve as recommendations and get contact information if possible.

Knowledge Self-Assessment Questions

Questions	Responses
Depending on the path you have chosen post-release, on a scale of 1 to 10—with 1 meaning poorly and 10 meaning very well—how well do you understand the following? _____Community college _____Certifications _____Vocational school _____Full-time employment (Who is hiring?) _____Entrepreneurship (What are you qualified to do?) _____Finances/budget (How well do you understand this?) _____Technology (How knowledgeable are you?)	
Once you have completed the list, decide where to start. What is the first action step to increase your knowledge?	
What is your plan to gain more knowledge? Write out the plan and be ready to share it with your mentor. This is a crucial conversation.	

Questions	Responses
In what way do you learn best? _____Auditory (hearing) _____Visual (seeing) _____Tactile-kinesthetic(doing/being hands on) _____Online _____Face-to-face _____Research on own _____Books _____Podcasts _____Workshops _____Classes	
Have you completed the following? _____Application exercise _____Create a functional resume _____Get proof of education or certifications _____Create a list of three people who could serve as references (letters could come from a chaplain, friend, or past employer—make sure they are on stationery)	
How can you become ready after you are released from prison?	

Knowledge Mentor Questions

Questions to ask the mentee:	Write out the mentee's responses.
Depending on the path you have chosen post-release, on a scale of 1 to 10—with 1 meaning poorly and 10 meaning very well—how well do you understand the following? _____Community college _____Certifications _____Vocational school _____Full-time employment (Who is hiring?) _____Entrepreneurship (What are you qualified to do?) _____Finances/budget (How well do you understand this?) _____Technology (How knowledgeable are you?)	
Once you have completed the list, decide where to start. What is the first action step to increase your knowledge?	
What is your plan to gain more knowledge? Write out the plan and be ready to share it with your mentor. This is a crucial conversation.	

Questions to ask the mentee:	Write out the mentee's responses.
In what way do you learn best? _____Auditory (hearing) _____Visual (seeing) _____Tactile-kinesthetic (doing/being hands on) _____Online _____Face-to-face _____Research on own _____Books _____Podcasts _____Workshops _____Classes	
What resources are available to acquire new knowledge?	
Have you completed the following? _____Application exercise _____Create a functional resume _____Get proof of education or certifications _____Create a list of three people who could serve as references	
How can you become ready after you are released from prison?	
Assignment for next week:	
How are the daily behavior questions going?	

> *Learn from your mistakes.*
> —Proverbs 26:1–12

Do you know how you learn best? Do you love to learn? Do you have a passion for trying new things? Do you engage in learning new things both inside and outside of school? Do you look for ways to stretch your creative capacity and yourself? I often feel like a kid in the candy store regarding learning. I feel like there is not enough time to learn about everything I am interested in but in a good and stimulating way. I make the time because it changes me. It opens my mind to new possibilities. I use what I learn from new areas to bring back to work in my role and apply it. I learn from others and broaden my perspective. I take personal-development courses to uncover my bias or understand my thinking more effectively.

Learning does not even have to be formal. I take every opportunity to learn something. Here are three examples: A few years ago, I had a dental emergency, and my dentist was out of town. I went to a dentist my sister referred to me. They took care of the problem; they were highly professional. Soon they became my dentist because of how I was treated. What impressed me most was how they made notes each time I was there. I am not talking about notes about my teeth, which would be expected. Their records were comprehensive, and the notes included whatever we talked about, whether that was family, job, or travel. It was like we picked up the conversation where it left off six months prior. I think this practice is brilliant. Wouldn't it be great if every customer-service operation did the same thing?

The second example is my website provider. Their customer service is spectacular. No one is happy when they call for tech support because it means they have a problem. The tech staff is patient and knowledgeable and has always resolved my issues 100 percent of the time. I share these two examples as I am always looking for excellent customer service experiences to bring it back to my operation and see how we can improve what we are doing. Where are you looking to learn?

The third example is my hairdresser. It is not a high-end salon, but every client is treated as a VIP. Every client is greeted when they walk through the door. They are called by name. The stylist works around the client's schedule, not the other way around. They strive to be on time. They offer water or coffee. They ask questions to make sure they deliver the best result. They take nothing for granted. They set up the next appointment before the client leaves. Can you imagine how each client feels when they leave the salon? What impression do you want to make?

If you like reading, there is an excellent resource by John R. DiJulius III (2003) titled *Secret Service: Hidden Systems That Deliver Unforgettable Customer Service*. This book shows you a variety of companies and the systems they use to offer exceptional customer service. As I mentioned, you can learn a lot by studying companies outside your field. What examples can you share related to what you have learned? What is one poor customer service experience you have encountered? How did that make you feel? You may find post-release that your job will be customer related, and thinking now about improving these skills can be helpful to your success.

Do you enjoy listening to webinars or podcasts? I love TED Talks on YouTube. If you are not familiar with TED, check it out. TED stands for Technology, Entertainment, and Design. These are eighteen-minute video talks by thought leaders who present high-quality information on trending topics. Check out TED talks about topics that interest you and can help your career. What three are your favorites?

Did you belong to professional associations before prison? Would learning a new language be helpful? Expand yourself. Do something different in a positive direction. Make a point of learning something new every day.

In addition to this week's article, read the short section in the back of the book called Now Hired, Now What, and be ready to discuss this with your mentor.

REFERENCES

DiJulius, John R., III. 2003. *Secret Service: Hidden Systems That Deliver Unforgettable Customer Service.* AMACOM.
TED (Technology, Entertainment, and Design): Ideas Worth Spreading. https://www.ted.com.

Learning Self-Assessment Questions

Questions	Responses
After reading the Career Development Tool Section, what did you complete?	
On a scale of 1 to 10, rate yourself with 1 being "I do not care to learn" and 10 being "I have a passion for learning." ____Love of learning	
What types of topics interest you?	
What was the last personal-development course you took?	
Have you watched TED Talks on YouTube? What are three of your favorites?	
What was the last book you read or listened to?	
What podcasts do you listen to? What type of music do you enjoy?	
Do you speak more than one language?	
What interests you?	
Where can lessons be learned from other industries?	
What customer service examples can you provide?	
How can you encourage others to be life-long learners?	
What did you learn from reading Now Hired, Now What?	

Learning Mentor Questions

Questions to ask the mentee:	Write out the mentee's responses.
After reading the Career Development Tool Section, what did you complete?	
How would you rate yourself on the topic of being a lifelong learner? Explain.	
What was the last personal-development course you took?	
What was the last book you read or listened to?	
Do you watch TED Talks? If yes, what is one of your favorites?	
What podcasts do you listen to? What type of music do you enjoy?	
Do you speak more than one language?	
What have you done to develop your creativity?	
What topics do you find less appealing, or what areas do you not like to learn about?	
How can you encourage others to be lifelong learners?	
Give me two examples of excellent customer service you have received.	
Give me one example of poor customer service you have received.	
What did you learn from reading Now Hired, Now What?	
Assignment for next week:	
How are the daily behavior questions going?	

> *The mind is everything. What you think, you become.*
> —Gautama Buddha

Do you have a fixed mindset or a growth mindset? How do you know? When you make a mistake, do you think you should stop or quit because you failed? Do you avoid risk and challenges? What do you tell yourself? When you are learning something new, and it is challenging and does not come quickly, what is your self-talk? Do you say to yourself, "It is something new to learn"? Do you want to be praised for the effort and the journey?

Mindset is defined as a set of attitudes one possesses. One of the best resources about mindset is Carol Dweck's book *Mindset: The New Psychology of Success; How We Can Fulfill Our Potential.* Read it and see how you can develop a growth mindset in all areas of your life. Dr. Carol Dweck describes a fixed mindset as being static, avoiding challenges, seeing the effort as fruitless, ignoring helpful negative feedback, and feeling threatened by the success of others. She then describes the characteristics of a growth mindset. These include "a desire to learn, embraces challenges, is persistent, learns from criticism, and is inspired by others." Which are you?

Carol Dweck's book challenged me to examine what I was saying to my students. I realized that many positive things I was voicing were creating a fixed mindset. I had to reframe the way I praised my students for their progress. I now applaud the effort, strategies, hard work, progress, persistence, and ability to learn from mistakes. I stopped saying "good job" or "you are so smart" as these are fixed ways of being. When I think about it now, my best learning came from my mistakes and not when I excelled.

I tested Carol Dweck's mindset theory for many years by facilitating a graduate new-student orientation workshop each session. We had a lot of interactive activities so the students could get an idea about what they were about to undertake in obtaining a master's degree. About midway through the orientation, I gave the graduate students an assignment. I told them that at our university, every student was expected to use the American Psychological Association (APA) formatting in referencing all the sources for their papers. I handed out a research paper to each student and had them try to find the APA errors. This was a tough assignment because they had not even started their classes. I watched with intrigue how they approached the task. Most took the paper and tried to figure something out. A few took the paper and threw it in total frustration. I did not let the exercise go for more than two minutes for fear of them leaving before they started. I then conducted a debrief or after-action review. I asked them how they felt when I handed out the assignment. Some said they were scared. Some were open to trying, and some said they felt like quitting. I told them to realize that they were in graduate school to learn new things. I told them I did not expect them to be able to do the assignment. I asked them to remember their feelings when we did this throughout their graduate-school journey.

I wanted to create a growth mindset for every person in the workshop. They would not need graduate school if they knew how to do these things. It is a place to learn, be challenged, and make mistakes. I then handed out an APA guide to help them do the assignment. We then reviewed the paper, and I noted the APA errors.

As I explained the difference and my intention, the students relaxed. They stated it was a lesson they would never forget. So how do you approach new things, and what do you say to yourself?

Biglifejournal.com created a set of questions to help you reframe your mindset:

- "What did you do today that made you think hard?"
- "What new strategies did you try?"
- "What mistake did you make that taught you something?"
- "What did you try that was hard today?"

Let us take this to the world of work. What is your mindset? Employees often say, "These people do not like me." People say, "My boss is making me do...." I have heard, "You cannot get ahead here because..." I have never said those things as I do not see the world that way. It is not my mindset or my self-talk. Indeed, there are workplaces where this exists, but is it that way, or is it a fixed mindset to justify your situation and make them wrong? Be mindful of your thinking. Indeed, you are the only person who knows. As you read this, you may take issue with me; however, a coach challenges your thinking.

REFERENCES

Biglifejournal.com

Dweck, Carol. 2007. *Mindset: The New Psychology of Success; How We Can Fulfill Our Potential*. New York: Ballantine Books.

Mindset Self-Assessment Questions

Questions	Responses
Overall, do you feel like you have a growth or fixed mindset?	
In what areas of your life do you have a growth mindset?	
In what areas of your life do you have a fixed mindset?	
Do you like to be rewarded for the outcome or the journey?	
What do you say to yourself when things are hard, or you are learning something for the first time?	
How can you begin to shift your mindset to a growth mindset?	
How will you know you are starting to shift your perspective?	
Be ready to discuss the pathway you have chosen with your mentor. Start mapping out a plan and time frame for accomplishing them over the next thirteen weeks.	

Mindset Mentor Questions

Questions to ask the mentee:	Write out the mentee's responses.
Describe what you think a growth mindset is.	
Describe what you think a fixed mindset is.	
Do you feel like you have a growth mindset or a fixed mindset?	
In what areas of your life do you have a growth mindset?	
In what areas of your life do you have a fixed mindset?	
Do you like to be rewarded for the outcome or the journey? Explain.	
What do you say to yourself when things are hard, or you are learning something for the first time?	
How can you begin to shift your mindset to a growth mindset?	
How will you know you are starting to shift your perspective?	

Questions to ask the mentee:	Write out the mentee's responses.
How can I encourage your growth in this area?	
We are halfway through the twenty-six traits. What do you feel you have learned thus far?	
How do you feel you have changed?	
What do you want to focus on for the next thirteen weeks to ensure you have developed a solid post-release plan?	
Assignment for next week:	
How are the daily behavior questions going?	

> *Let no corrupting talk come out of your mouths, but only such as is good for building up, as fits the occasion, that it may give grace to those you hear.*
> —Ephesians 4:29

What is new-media literacy? According to IGI Global (2020), it is the ability to use new-media tools and digital technology to compute and solve problems to function in a job, in life, and society. It is one of the most sought-after skills in 2021 by employers. Given the limitations to access technology, this will present quite a challenge for you being incarcerated. It is not impossible, though. You can read about it. You can ask your mentor about it. You can take advantage of certification programs offered in prison.

If you have been incarcerated for the past 10 years, you will likely notice significant changes in technology upon your release. Here are some key advancements that have occurred in the past decade:

- Smartphone Revolution: The proliferation of smartphones (cell phones) has had a profound impact on society. These devices have become an essential part of every-day life, providing instant access to information, communication, entertainment, and various services.
- Social Media and Communication: Social media platforms such as Facebook, Insta-gram, Twitter, and Snapchat have experienced massive growth, transforming how people connect, share information, and engage with others globally.
- Streaming Services: Streaming platforms like Netflix, Hulu, and Amazon Prime have revolutionized how people consume entertainment. Streaming services offer on-demand access to a vast library of movies, TV shows, and original content, replacing traditional cable TV.
- Artificial Intelligence (AI) and Virtual Assistants: AI has become more prominent, with virtual assistants like Apple's Siri, Google Assistant, and Amazon's Alexa becoming part of people's daily lives. These assistants can perform tasks, answer questions, and control smart home devices.
- E-commerce and Online Shopping: Online shopping has boomed, with major play-ers like Amazon dominating the market. The convenience of shopping from home and the growth of platforms like Shopify have transformed the retail landscape.

- Internet of Things (IoT): The number of connected devices in everyday life has increased dramatically. Smart homes, wearable devices, and IoT applications in areas such as healthcare, transportation, and agriculture have become more prevalent.
- Advancements in Mobile Apps: Mobile apps have soared in popularity, with nearly every industry offering apps for various purposes. From ride-sharing (Uber, Lyft) to food delivery (Uber Eats, DoorDash), there are countless apps that have changed the way people access services.
- Advancements in Biotechnology and Healthcare: The last decade witnessed breakthroughs in biotechnology, including gene editing technologies like CRISPR-Cas9, advancements in personalized medicine, and the integration of digital healthcare solutions for better patient care such as video visits.
- Rise of Video Conferencing and Remote Work: With the recent global events, video conferencing platforms like Zoom, Microsoft Teams, and Google Meet have become essential for remote work, education, and online meetings.
- Increased Cybersecurity Concerns: Cybersecurity threats, online scams, and data breaches have become more prevalent. Organizations and individuals are now placing more emphasis on cybersecurity measures and data protection.

These are just some of the major technological changes that have occurred over the past decade. Upon your release, you may find these advancements both exciting and overwhelming, but they also present new opportunities and possibilities for personal and professional growth.

Most jobs today require high levels of skill in accessing information, conducting research, solving problems, and working collaboratively (Roscorla 2020). Many industries will not hire you depending on the nature of your crime. It is best to research companies that will hire someone with a criminal record. It is better to be prepared. What resources are available to you? How can your mentor help in this area? If you are still connected with your family or friends, what can they teach you? Sometimes the younger the person, the more proficient they are with media and digital technology as our school systems demand it as they prepare them for the future. It is common today for grandparents and parents to ask their kids for help. There is nothing to be embarrassed about. We cannot be experts in everything.

Media literacy is understanding different types of media and the message they are sending. Examples of media literacy include text messages, AI chatbots, memes, viral videos, social media, video games, advertising, etc. How does this help?

Once you begin to learn about new media, it can help you think critically. It will help you become a more intelligent consumer with the help of your mentor and people around you, like your teachers, family, and friends. You can begin to recognize specific points of view, like the creator or author of the media. It is not just understanding the media but being able to think critically.

A joke has been around for the last few years, and it goes like this: Someone is talking about something they read on the internet, and they say, "I read it on the internet, so it must be true." Nothing could be further from the truth.

This is where you need to think critically. What is the message they are trying to send? Is it a trustworthy source? How did the message make you feel? What is the purpose of the message? Do you agree or disagree, and why? Does the message appeal to emotions or facts?

REFERENCES

IGI Global. 2020. "What Is New Media Literacy?" https://www.igi-global.com/dictionary/new-media-literacy/20287#:~:text=The%20ability%20to%20critically%20and,in%20social%20and%20cultural%20contexts.

Roscorla, T. 2020. "10 Steps to Strengthen Digital and Media Literacy" (November 14). https://www.govtech.com/education/news/10-Steps-to-Strengthen-Digital-and-Media-Literacy.html.

New-Media Literacy Self-Assessment Questions

Questions	Responses
What do you know about new media and digital technology?	
What changes listed in the article are new to you?	
Where do you want to start learning about this topic?	
What do you know about computers?	
What do you know about cell phones?	
What do you know about websites?	
What do you know about podcasts?	
What do you know about Facebook?	
What do you know about LinkedIn?	
What do you know about AI chatbots?	
What companies hire people with criminal records?	
What jobs are off-limits to people who have a criminal record?	
What concerns do you have about new-media literacy?	

New-Media Literacy Mentor Questions

Questions to ask the mentee:	Write out the mentee's responses.
What do you know about new media and digital technology?	
What changes listed in the article are new to you?	
Where do you want to start learning?	
What do you know about computers?	
What do you know about cell phones?	
What do you know about websites?	
What do you know about podcasts?	
What do you know about Facebook?	
What do you know about LinkedIn?	
What do you know about AI chatbots?	
What companies hire people with criminal records?	
What jobs are off-limits to people who have a criminal record?	
What concerns do you have about new-media literacy?	
How can I support you?	
Assignment for next week:	
How are the daily behavior questions going?	

 **IS FOR OPPORTUNITY**

> *So then, as we have opportunity, let us do good to*
> *everyone, and especially to those who are*
> *of the household of faith.*
> —Galatians 6:10

Be observant. Look for opportunities to contribute and make a difference. When problems are presented, think through how to bring value instead of complaining.

One of the best examples of this happened when I started my career in higher education as a new faculty member. I taught at this school for three months before the fall session. The department director told me my class in the fall session started at 7:00 a.m. So, on the first day of class, I arrived early, set up my class, and by 7:10 a.m., no students were in class. I thought it strange and headed to the registrar's office to see the course schedule. The schedule said my class started at 9:00 a.m., not 7:00 a.m. I decided to just wait in the faculty/staff lounge until class was to begin. It was the best two hours I have ever spent. As each new faculty member entered the lounge, they would ask me where to turn in attendance sheets, how to use the copy machine, where the mailboxes were, the class schedule, the registrar's office location, etc. I helped everyone even though I was new and did not know everything.

I went to teach my class at 9:00 a.m. The class ended at noon. I promptly went to the Dean of Education's office and asked to speak with him. I had only met him once, and I was nervous. His assistant said he had time to see me. I explained what had occurred that morning. I explained how many new teachers were unsure of what to do on the first day of class. I told him that in my previous role in the hospitality industry, we always held a new-employee orientation before anyone started. It helped them feel better connected and more confident in the position. He said, "Great idea. You should do that." I laughed to myself as I had not been given an orientation but said, "Yes, I would be happy to do this." I knew I needed to partner with someone at the school who knew the building, programs, and all the floors. I found that person in Cliff Willson. I asked him if he would help, and he said yes. So, we held the new-employee orientation each quarter for the following two years. Each time we delivered the orientation, it became better. I could have complained about the situation but chose a different approach. This situation propelled me and led me to some of the most amazing opportunities in higher education over the next seventeen years.

Think about the problems you see in life. Reframe problems as opportunities and see where your life and career take you.

Opportunity Self-Assessment Questions

Questions	Responses
What problems or gaps have you noticed that could be viewed as opportunities?	
When have you taken the initiative to bring solutions to your family, classes, or prison? Provide three examples: 1. 2. 3.	
What kind of impact do you want to make?	
How will you know you are making progress?	

Opportunity Mentor Questions

Questions to ask the mentee:	Write out the mentee's responses.
Did the example shared change your perspective?	
What problems or gaps have you noticed that could be viewed as opportunities?	
When have you taken the initiative to bring solutions to your family, classes, or prison? Provide three examples: 1. 2. 3.	
What kind of impact do you want to make?	
What is one action you can take to improve in this area?	
How will you measure your improvement in this area?	
How can I support you?	
Assignment for next week:	
How are the daily behavior questions going?	

P IS FOR POST-TRAUMATIC STRESS DISORDER

> *If any of you lacks wisdom, let him ask God,*
> *who gives generously to all without reproach,*
> *and it will be given to him.*
>
> —James 1:5

Post-traumatic stress disorder is a mental condition that may occur in people who have experienced or witnessed a highly traumatic event such as sexual violence, incarceration, military service, or surviving a natural disaster. While most people will experience a traumatic event in their lifetime, not everyone develops PTSD, and researchers are unsure why some do and some do not. (Hall, K. M., 2021, GoodRxHealth).

Triggers are specific events, situations, or stimuli that remind someone of a past traumatic experience and can elicit a strong emotional or physiological response. Coping with PTSD (post-traumatic stress disorder) after incarceration can be challenging. Triggers are usually associated with your senses, such as sight, sound, or smell. Also, not having enough social support can worsen triggers.

According to GoodRxHealth, specific triggers set off PTSD symptoms. They are panic, medical care, loud sounds, emotional pain, words, style or tone of voice, angry voices, physical traits, music, touch, objects, similar places, time of day, age reminders, arguments, loss of a loved one, and even colors. (Hall, 2021, pg. 6-8).

Recognize triggers: What are your triggers? Work with your loved one to identify specific stimuli, such as loud noises, flashbacks, nightmares, intrusive thoughts, trouble sleeping, angry outbursts, mood changes, or confinement that remind them of their traumatic experience. Understanding these triggers can help avoid or manage them proactively.

There are ways to cope with PTSD. When triggered, you can start with deep breathing techniques, meditation, muscle relaxation exercises, listening to soothing music, and getting in touch with nature. In addition, you can use grounding exercises to focus your senses. GoodRxHealth (2021) recommends the following:

- Name five things you can see right now (bedroom wall).
- Name four things you can feel right now (breeze on your skin).
- Name three things you can hear (such as music playing).
- Name two things you can smell (like your cologne).
- Name one thing you can taste right now (such as any aftertaste of grapefruit).

Other examples can include:

- Petting a furry animal.
- Holding ice in your hands.
- Running warm water over your hands.
- Squishing a stress ball.
- Sucking on sour candy.

Here are some strategies and ways that family and friends can offer support. They are:

- Understand and educate yourself: Learn about PTSD and its symptoms to better understand what your loved one is experiencing. This can help you be more empathetic and supportive.
- Be patient and non-judgmental: Reassure your loved one that triggers are normal and that you are there to support them. Encourage open communication and let them express their feelings without judgment or criticism.
- Create a safe environment: Help your loved one feel safe and secure by creating a calm and supportive environment. Make sure they have a quiet space to retreat to when needed and establish routines that promote stability.
- Encourage professional help: Suggest that your loved one seek professional help from a therapist or counselor experienced in treating PTSD or support groups. Therapy can provide them with coping strategies and tools to manage their symptoms effectively.
- Offer practical support: Assisting with daily tasks or responsibilities can alleviate stress or triggers for your loved one. This could involve helping with transportation, accompanying them to appointments, or assisting with job or housing searches.
- Practice self-care: Encourage your loved one to engage in self-care activities that promote relaxation and reduce symptoms, such as exercise, meditation, or hobbies they enjoy.
- Provide emotional support: Be there to listen and validate their experiences. Offer a shoulder to lean on and remind them they are not alone in their healing journey.

Remember, every individual's experience with PTSD is unique, so it is essential to adapt your support and strategies to their specific needs. If necessary, seek professional help or join support groups tailored to your situation.

REFERENCES

National Alliance on Mental Illness
National Center for PTSD

PTSD Self-Assessment Questions

Questions	Responses
Do you feel you have PTSD?	
What are some of your triggers?	
What coping strategies can or do you use?	
How can you help your family and friends understand PTSD and help you when you are released?	
What is your plan for dealing with this when you are released?	

PTSD Mentor Questions

Questions to ask the mentee:	Write out the mentee's responses.
Do you feel you have PTSD?	
What are some of your triggers?	
What coping strategies can or do you use?	
How can you help your family and friends understand PTSD and help you when you are released?	
What is your plan for dealing with this when you are released?	
How can I support you?	
Assignment for next week:	
How are the daily behavior questions going?	

> *So few grow because so few study.*
> —D. L. Moody, Pleasure, and Profit in Bible Study

The art of asking questions seems to dwindle due to the fast pace of business. Asking questions will save you time and give you the information you need to make informed decisions. This is true when seeking employment, learning something new, or getting to know someone. Employers often close an interview by asking, "Do you have any questions?" You should have at least two questions prepared in advance to be ready when they ask.

Ask questions. Questions provide answers. They inform. Questions are information disguised as power. The more you ask, the more you learn about people, processes, plans, and passion. The more questions you ask, the more attractive you become. It is not in what you know; it is what you learn. If this is an area of weakness for you, learn how to ask essential questions.

There are specific types of questions for different situations. The art of asking and answering questions was used to stimulate critical thinking as far back as Socrates (470–339 BC). Asking questions helps inform and educate.

Now it is time to prepare your interview questions for finding employment. You can practice before your session with your mentor and before going to an interview, whether you are still in prison and employers come to the site, or you are out on your own.

Second Chance Center lists ten interview questions and how to respond. They are:

1. Tell me about yourself. (This can be a tricky question. Talk about your highlights [two minutes] and past work experiences. Don't spend twenty minutes telling your life story.)
2. Why should we hire you? (Make sure you discuss how your strengths match the position, not because you need a job or are desperate. This may be true, but you cannot let it show.)
3. What is your greatest strength? What is your greatest weakness?
4. Why do you want to work here?
5. Tell me how your skills are a match for this job.
6. When you were employed, why did you leave your last job?
7. What is your greatest accomplishment?
8. Describe a difficult work situation and what you did to overcome it.
9. Where do you see yourself in five years?
10. Do you have any questions for me?

According to Jobcast by Indeed (October 2, 2020), here are some sample behavior-based questions. Practice how you might answer:

- Tell me about a time when you handled a challenging situation. What happened, and what was the result?
- Tell me about a time when you made a mistake. How did you handle it?
- Tell me about how you work under pressure.
- Give me an example of how you set goals.
- Tell me about a time you were angry, how you handled it, and what the outcome was.
- Share an example of how you have helped motivate another person.
- Often at the end of the interview, the employers expect you to ask a few questions. Typical questions you might ask are as follows:
  - Can you describe a typical day in this position?
  - To whom will I be reporting?
  - What do you like about working here?
  - What do you find challenging working here?
  - When will you decide, and how will you notify me?

Discussing Criminal History: The Challenging Questions

How do I answer questions about incarceration?

There are many ways to handle this situation. The Second Chance Center recommends five possible approaches. Regardless, write out what you want to share. Practice your response. Don't leave your reply to chance.

1. When applying for a job, you might want to attach a statement about your criminal background and then talk with the hiring manager about the job you are applying for and how you are qualified.
2. In the interview, when asked, "Tell me about yourself," talk about your strengths and how you are a good fit for the job. Add something like, "In addition to these experiences, I would like to take the time to share something more personal about myself" (share your prepared statement).
3. Be prepared to share what you learned while incarcerated and how you have changed.
4. Another way to reveal your past is when the employer asks about your greatest weakness. Give your prepared statement.
5. At the end of the interview, when the employer has asked all their questions, and you have asked your questions, say something like, "Before I leave today, there is something I would like you to know." Then tell the employer your prepared statement.
6. The interview is over. You did a great job, and they extended an offer. This is the time to accept the offer but disclose to the employer your criminal background. Share with them your prepared statement.

When discussing your criminal background, be honest, but soften how you present it.

Examples:
- o I was in possession of a controlled substance.
- o I was using my body as a means of earning a living.
- o I was in a verbal/physical confrontation, and as a result, someone lost their life.
- o I helped someone during a crime that took place.
- o I had unauthorized possession of a firearm.
- o I used my authority/access to take money/property that did not belong to me.

Are-You-Ready Checklist

- ☐ What is your confidence level? Your mindset? Your energy level?
- ☐ Résumé—take a copy for all people interviewing you.
- ☐ Bring two pens with black ink.
- ☐ Bring some note-taking paper (a spiral notebook is an option).
- ☐ Know in advance how to get to the location (give yourself ample time to get there at least fifteen minutes early).
- ☐ Take your driver's license/ID card and Social Security card.
- ☐ Produce your letters of recommendation (if asked).
- ☐ Produce your list of references (including complete contact information—name, address, phone number, and email address; include personal and professional references).
- ☐ Research the company in advance—go online.
- ☐ Practice interviewing.
- ☐ Be professionally dressed.
- ☐ Go to the interview alone.
- ☐ Turn off your cell phone; do not take beverages or food into the interview. Do not smoke or chew gum.
- ☐ Get a good night's sleep the night before.
- ☐ Have a firm handshake, but not too strong.
- ☐ Maintain eye contact.
- ☐ Remember the interviewer's name and ask if you can have their card when you leave.
- ☐ Take only the essentials and be organized.

REFERENCES

Second Chance Program
https://nationalreentryresourcecenter.org/second-chance-act

Questioning Self-Assessment Questions

Questions	Responses
Review the interview questions and write your answers.	
Have you ever thought about the types of questions you ask? What will they be?	
How will you respond to the challenging questions about your time incarcerated?	
Review the checklist in this section. How prepared do you feel? What are your concerns? Write them down.	

Questioning Mentor Questions

Questions to ask the mentee:	Write out the mentee's responses.
Review the interview questions and write your answers.	
Have you ever thought about the types of questions you ask? What will they be?	
How will you respond to the challenging questions about your time incarcerated?	
Review the checklist in this section. How prepared do you feel? What are your concerns? Write them down.	
How can I support you in questioning?	
Assignment for next week:	Read the Career Development Tool Section. Complete the following: Application Exercise Functional Resume Proof of Education/Certifications Create a list of Recommendations/References
How are the daily behavior questions going?	

> *Let us not be surprised when we have to face difficulties. When the wind blows hard on a tree, the roots stretch and grow the stronger; let it be so with us. Let us not be weaklings yielding to every wind that blows, but strong in the spirit to resist.*
>
> —Amy Carmichael

According to Greitens (2016), in his incredible book on resilience, resilience is the virtue that enables people to move through hardship and become better (p. 3). Examples include veterans who come home with lost limbs or PTSD. Greitens, a former Navy SEAL, understands what being on the front line means, where battles are fought, and fates decided, and not everyone understands.

It includes people who have lost loved ones, suffered from a terminal disease, or a friend or family member who committed suicide. It can consist of job or financial loss and issues with health and well-being. It can include losing your freedom.

Greitens (2016, 5) states pain can make or break you. He shares what worked for him and his Navy SEAL brothers and has worked overtime. These are questions to focus on: How do you focus your mind, control your stress, and excel under pressure? How do you work through fear and build courage? How do you overcome defeat and rise above obstacles?

I live by several sayings I have made up to continue to move forward. One that serves me well is, "Circumstances do not define me." When things seem low, I cannot focus on the moment and must look forward. I remember to, "Let go and let God." You can turn hardship into victory, but it is not easy. You have a choice. Are you going to let the current circumstance defeat you? Remember, God is in control. No one gets through life without a struggle, which is a good thing to remember when going through incredible challenges.

Resilience is the key to having a well-lived life and being able to navigate changes and not resist them. Some of my most painful experiences in life have been the most significant learning and growth opportunities. I did not know when it was happening, but I can look back and see how far I have come.

REFERENCES

Greitens, E. 2016. *Resilience*. New York: First Mariner Books.

Resiliency Self-Assessment Questions

Questions	Responses
Who are people you admire for their resiliency?	
What brings you happiness?	
Who are you?	
What habits serve you?	
How do you navigate challenging times?	
What is your purpose?	
What do you need to take responsibility for?	
How do you deal with pain and loss?	
What are some examples of your resiliency?	

Resiliency Mentor Questions

Questions to ask the mentee:	Write out the mentee's responses.
Who are people you admire for their resiliency?	
What brings you happiness?	
Who are you?	
What habits serve you?	
How do you navigate challenging times?	
What is your purpose?	
What do you need to take responsibility for?	
How do you deal with pain and loss?	
What are some examples of your resiliency?	
Assignment for next week:	
How are the daily behavior questions going?	

S IS FOR SELF-AWARENESS

> *Knowing yourself is key to all wisdom.*
> —Aristotle, ancient Greek philosopher

Self-awareness is vital to your success. If you know yourself, you get it. Have you looked in the mirror lately? How self-aware are you? Do you know where your blind spots are? Can you identify your strengths? Do you know your weaknesses? If you want to improve your self-awareness, here are some approaches.

Based on the last few months of learning and growing, it is time to stretch yourself. Consider conducting your 360-degree assessment. Find five to seven people whom you trust to give you honest feedback but who are not friends who will just tell you what you want to hear. Ask them the following: (1) three of your strength areas, (2) two areas that need to be developed, (3) one thing they find frustrating about you, (4) their wish for you, (5) an area of your expertise, (6) your blind spots, and (7) how you can improve and challenge yourself. Write down what they tell you. You will be amazed at what you learn about yourself. Remember, feedback is a gift.

After you did this exercise, what did you learn?

I recently asked a few professional friends what their managers think of them. I asked, "How do you think your teachers or managers think about how you present yourself?" How would they describe your personality traits and leadership style? Tone? Nonverbal expressions? Time-management ability? Are you a team player? Problem-solver? Respectful? Contributor? What is your communication style, personality, etc.?

They said they had no idea. Not knowing is a huge problem. If you do not understand what people around you are thinking, how will you ever be able to improve?

Self-Awareness Self-Assessment Questions

Questions	Responses
What did you learn from the interviews you conducted?	
What are three of your strength areas?	
What are two areas that need to be developed?	
What is one thing they find frustrating about you?	
What do they wish for you?	
What is an area where you excel?	
What are your blind spots?	
How can you improve and challenge yourself?	

Self-Awareness Mentor Questions

Questions to ask the mentee:	Write out the mentee's responses.
Based on the interviews you conducted, what did you learn?	
Based on the interviews you conducted, what surprised you?	
Have you taken any online self-awareness assessments? If yes, what did you learn or confirm?	
Have you ever taken any personal-development courses to discover your blind spots? If so, what classes? What did you find out?	
What traits are essential to getting a job or fulfilling your goals?	
How can I support you in your quest for self-assessment?	
Assignment for next week:	
How are the daily behavior questions going?	

T IS FOR THANK YOU

> *Give thanks to the Lord with all your heart.*
> —Psalms 9:1

When was the last time you said, "Thank you"? Those two words are the most important words for your life and career. When was the last time you wrote a handwritten thank-you note? You might think this is old school, but the impression you make by doing this speaks volumes. The fact that you are taking the time to acknowledge someone means a great deal.

Think about opportunities to say *thank you*. Did your mentor give you some solid advice? Did you seek a job recommendation? Did someone help you with a letter of recommendation? Did you go out for a job interview? Did you write a follow-up *thank you*? Were you given a job? Did you say *thank you*? Were you given a promotion? Did you say *thank you*? Did you thank your team members when they completed a project on time? Were you given a bonus? Did you say *thank you*? You might be thinking, "Hey, I earned it. What's the big deal?" That attitude is *entitlement*. How about being grateful and saying *thank you* instead? When was the last time you said *thank you* to a family member?

Did a co-worker take the time to help you out? Did someone remember your birthday or work anniversary? Did someone take you to coffee, lunch, or dinner, and they paid? Did someone drive you to a meeting? Did you say *thank you*? When was the last time you thanked your boss?

As you can see from the above examples, there are ample opportunities to say *thank you*. If this is not your strong suit, schedule a reminder on your calendar to do this at least weekly. Try it and see what happens! Make this a habit each week.

Thank You Self-Assessment Questions

Questions	Responses
Where have you noticed opportunities to say *thank you*?	
Have you noticed missed opportunities to say *thank you*?	
How does it make you feel when you say or write a thank-you note?	
Does this come naturally?	
Do you need to schedule a reminder on your calendar?	
How important is it to say *thank you* in life and business?	

Thank-You Mentor Questions

Questions to ask the mentee:	Write out the mentee's responses.
A statement is often quoted: "Employees do not quit organizations; they quit people." What does this mean to you?	
What kind of person, employee, or leader do you want to be?	
How important is it that employees and team members feel appreciated?	
What makes you feel appreciated at work?	
Where have you noticed opportunities to say *thank you*?	
Have you noticed missed opportunities to say *thank you*?	
How important in business do you think it is to say *thank you*?	
How can I further support you in developing your "thank-you" muscle?	
Assignment for next week:	
How are the daily behavior questions going?	

U IS FOR UNDERSTANDING

> *For the Lord gives wisdom, from His mouth comes knowledge and understanding.*
> —Proverbs 2:6

Understanding is "being able to comprehend or be aware of other people's feelings and thoughts" (*Oxford Dictionary*). How do you become more understanding? Think about someone in your life who is understanding. Who are they? What qualities do they possess?

If you're not sure where to start, Dr. Dorsay's (2020) three-step method for developing understanding can help you get started.

Step one is to bring empathy to all your interactions. Empathy is putting yourself in the other person's shoes but not walking in them. It starts with you. He suggests that when trying to understand someone's motivations, saying, "I never thought of it that way," or asking, "What makes you think that?" are good ways to move to mutual understanding. Listen actively. Look past first impressions. Recognize that most people are self-centered, not cruel. Pay attention to body language to better understand a person's mood and intentions. Understand that most people have the same thoughts, fears, and hopes (Dorsay 2020).

Step two is to understand other cultures and regions. Cultural influences can be complicated. Learn about history. Leave your existing biases and ideas at the door. We all have biases, whether conscious or unconscious. Share part of your culture to encourage others to share theirs. Learn about other cultures through reading or watching television (Dorsay 2020).

Step three is to understand yourself. Make learning a priority in everything you do. Consider your goals to figure out where you want to go. Ask yourself how you handle stress. Be open and upfront in your interactions. Be authentic. Honestly examine the root of your biases. Embrace the truth that you will never know everything about yourself, and that is okay. Continue evaluating and thinking about yourself throughout your life (Dorsay 2020).

What are you taking away from this chapter?

REFERENCES

Dorsay, A. 2020. "How to Be Understanding" (November 11). https://www.wikihow.com/Be-Understanding.

"Understanding." *Oxford Dictionary*.

Understanding Self-Assessment Questions

Questions	Responses
How can you show empathy?	
How can you demonstrate active listening?	
How can you look past first impressions?	
How effective are you at recognizing body language? Explain.	
How often do you think about how you would feel if you were in another person's position?	
How knowledgeable are you about different cultures?	
Before incarceration, where did you travel? What did you learn when you left your hometown?	
What known biases do you have?	
What are you proud of regarding your heritage?	
How often do you ask people what TV shows, movies, or music they like? It is a way to bond and get to know one another. What has your experience been like when asking? What have you learned?	

Questions	Responses
How can you learn about differences going forward? The world is a diverse place.	
Where do you think your biases were learned?	
How can you keep an open mind?	
How have you changed? How have you stayed the same?	

Understanding Mentor Questions

Questions to ask the mentee:	Write out the mentee's responses.
How do you show empathy?	
How do you demonstrate active listening?	
How do you look past first impressions?	
How effective are you at recognizing body language? Explain.	
How often do you think about how you would feel if you were in their position?	
How knowledgeable are you about different cultures?	
Before incarceration, where did you travel? What did you learn when you left your hometown?	
What known biases do you have?	
What are you proud of regarding your heritage?	
How often do you ask people what TV shows, movies, or music they like? It is a way to bond and get to know one another. What has your experience been like when asking? What have you learned?	

Questions to ask the mentee:	Write out the mentee's responses.
How can you learn about differences going forward? The world is a diverse place.	
Where do you think your biases were learned?	
How can you keep an open mind?	
How have you changed? How have you stayed the same?	
Assignment for next week:	
How are the daily behavior questions going?	

V IS FOR VICTORIES

> *I wait quietly before God, for my victory comes from Him.*
> —Psalms 62:1

The behavior chapter and Dr. Marshall Goldsmith's approach show the importance of looking forward, not backward. We must focus on victories and not dwell on setbacks, disappointments, or faults. Negativity drains you. Pastor Ray Patrick (September 3, 2019) says it can steal your confidence and joy. How can you get into the habit of focusing on victories?

Pastor Patrick encourages all of us to get into the habit of focusing on victories. He says, "Remember, every good and perfect gift comes from God. As you praise and thank Him for His victories in your life, He will pour His blessings on you. He will open supernatural doors for you to move forward in strength, to fulfill the dreams and desires He has placed in your heart!"

Whatever you focus on, you get more of it. It is your choice. One way I keep myself inspired is through quotes. I am going to share a few people I follow to stay motivated:

Joyce Meyer said, "No matter what happened to you in the past or what is going on in your life right now, it has no power to keep you from having an amazingly good life if you walk by faith in God. God loves you! He wants you to live with victory over sin so you can possess His promises for your life today."

Joel Osteen said, "If you want success, if you want wisdom, if you want to be prosperous and healthy, you are going to have to do more than meditate and believe. You must boldly declare words of faith and victory over yourself and your family."

Nelson Mandela said, "Education is the most powerful way to change the world."

Maya Angelou said, "We may encounter many defeats, but we must not be defeated."

Billy Graham said, "Begin to live as if your prayers have already been answered."

What quotes keep you inspired to live a life of victory?

REFERENCES

Patrick, R. 2019. "Time to Focus on Your Victories and Not Your Past Failures" (November 11). https://godinterest.com/2019/09/03/time-to-focus-on-your-victories-and-not-your-past-failures/.

Victories Self-Assessment Questions

Questions	Responses
What do you think of what Pastor Patrick shared?	
"I wait quietly before God, for my victory comes from him" (Psalms 62:1). What does this mean to you?	
Joyce Meyer said, "No matter what happened to you in the past or what is going on in your life right now, it has no power to keep you from having an amazingly good life if you walk by faith in God. God loves you! He wants you to live with victory over sin so you can possess His promises for your life today." What does this mean to you?	
Joel Osteen said, "If you want success, if you want wisdom, if you want to be prosperous and healthy, you are going to have to do more than meditate and believe. You must boldly declare words of faith and victory over yourself and your family." What do you think?	
Nelson Mandela said, "Education is the most powerful way to change the world." How do you feel about this quote?	

Questions	Responses
Maya Angelou said, "We may encounter many defeats, but we must not be defeated." How can you apply this to your life?	
Billy Graham said, "Begin to live as if your prayers have already been answered." How can this quote inspire you going forward?	
What quotes keep you inspired to live victoriously?	

Victories Mentor Questions

Questions to ask the mentee:	Write out the mentee's responses.
What do you think of what Pastor Patrick shared?	
"I wait quietly before God, for my victory comes from him" (Psalms 62:1). What does this mean to you?	
Joyce Meyer said, "No matter what happened to you in the past or what is going on in your life right now, it has no power to keep you from having an amazingly good sure if you walk by faith in God. God loves you! He wants you to live with victory over sin so you can possess His promises for your life today." What does this mean to you?	
Joel Osteen said, "If you want success, if you want wisdom, if you want to be prosperous and healthy, you will have to do more than meditate and believe; you must boldly declare words of faith and victory over yourself and your family." What do you think?	
Nelson Mandela said, "Education is the most powerful way to change the world." How do you feel about this quote?	

Questions to ask the mentee:	Write out the mentee's responses.
Maya Angelou said, "We may encounter many defeats, but we must not be defeated." How can you apply this to your life?	
Billy Graham said, "Begin to live as if your prayers have already been answered." How can this quote inspire you going forward?	
What quotes keep you inspired to live victoriously?	
Assignment for next week:	
How are the daily behavior questions going?	

W IS FOR WORK

> *Whatever you do work it with all your heart, as working for the Lord, not for human masters, since you know you will receive an inheritance from the Lord as a reward. It is the Lord Christ you are serving.*
> —Colossians 3:23–24

You are less likely to return to prison if you can find reliable employment. For most felons, any legitimate job is better than returning to prison. The truth is the job search will be frustrating at times. It is for everyone. But it is possible if you prepare and make the extra effort.

Before we begin, start to reflect on who you are. We have begun a journey together; it is time to bring it together. Having a job soon after you leave prison is critical in your road to success.

What have your learned? What are you proud of? What programs have you participated in to improve your skill level, education, or certification expertise while in prison? What skills and experience did you have pre-incarceration? What do you like doing? Given your skills and talents, what might be an ideal job for you? What job opportunities might be available for someone with a criminal record? What companies might be hiring? How will you find out? Who in your network can help?

Nonprofit and public organizations can help you get started, such as second chance programs in your area. Catholic charities, federal bonding programs, Clean Slate, and Unlocking Doors can help you get a fresh start.

Good felon-friendly jobs are available from the government and various companies. Ideally, you pursued a trade in prison. Millions of Americans have felony convictions. You know firsthand that jobs are not easy to come by, and it can seem daunting.

Companies like Goodwill, Ace Hardware, Alamo Rent a Car, Best Western, Comcast, trucking companies, Sprint, Dillard's, Embassy Suites, ExxonMobil, Goodyear, Jiffy Lube, Kohls, PetSmart, Olive Garden, Safeway, Walmart, and Xerox will hire felons, to name a few. Looking over the list, you see retail and hospitality are great places to start.

Educational opportunities, such as trade schools, community colleges, vocational programs, certifications, or universities, are great ways to enhance your earning potential. They do accept felons. There may be some majors you might not be able to pursue depending on the type of criminal background you have, but there are still plenty of choices. More and more jobs are going toward digital technology and working from home (Trade-Schools.net).

Potential careers could include the following:

- Barber
- Cook
- Customer service representative
- Commercial driver
- Construction worker
- Dog trainer
- Electrician
- Entrepreneur
- General laborer
- Glass installer
- Graphic designer
- HVAC technician
- Landscape worker
- Mechanic
- Mobile app developer
- Oil and gas entry-level position
- Painter
- Stock-order clerk
- Substance-abuse counselor
- Web designer
- Welder
- Wind technician
- Writer
- Motivational speaker
- Shipping and receiving clerk

The plan: Now that you have answered some questions, it is time to create the résumé, letter of recommendation, and references, decide what jobs you can apply for, and work through the readiness checklist.

REFERENCES

Rudd, L. 2020. "37 Jobs for Felons That Offer a Good Second Chance" (October 1). https://www.trade-schools.net/articles/jobs-for-felons.

Work Self-Assessment Questions

Questions	Responses
What have you learned?	
What are you proud of?	
What programs have you participated in to improve your skill level, education, or certification expertise while in prison?	
What skills or experience did you have pre-incarceration?	
What do you like doing?	
Given your skills and talents, what might be an ideal job for you?	
What job opportunities might be available for someone with a criminal record?	
What companies might be hiring?	
How will you find out?	
Who in your network can help?	

Work Self-Assessment Questions

Questions to ask the mentee:	Write out the mentee's responses.
What have you learned?	
What are you proud of?	
What programs have you participated in to improve your skill level, education, or certification expertise while in prison?	
What skills or experience did you have pre-incarceration?	
What do you like doing?	
Given your skills and talents, what might be an ideal job for you?	
What job opportunities might be available for someone with a criminal record?	
What companies might be hiring?	
How will you find out?	
Who in your network can help?	
Assignment for next week:	**Reading for next week:** Make a list of ideal jobs/careers.
How are the daily behavior questions going?	

> *There is neither Jew nor Greek, there is neither slave nor free, there is no male and female, for you are all in one in Christ Jesus.*
> —Galatians 3:28

The environment of a prison varies from one prison to another. The reality for many is racial tension, gangs, separatism, fear, concern for personal safety, and so much more. One of the more significant challenges you will find when you return to your hometown or a new environment is how much the world has changed. Younger people today believe in diversity, equity, and inclusion. You might have been exposed to this way of thinking before, but it is a competency that can be learned.

How can you learn more about cultural awareness? Are training or books available on the subject? Get to know each person without preconceptions. Recognize your biases and do not let them stop you from getting to know people.

Ask questions. Practice good manners; saying *please* and *thank you* go a long way. Learn about holidays and traditions with people from different backgrounds through conversations about holidays, food, and family traditions. Pay attention.

Preparing for life on the outside and developing an appreciation for cultural differences and diversity requires intentional effort and learning. Here are some strategies that can help individuals navigate these challenges:

- Education and exposure: Encourage individuals to engage in educational programs while incarcerated that promote awareness and understanding of different cultures, histories, and perspectives. This includes reading books, participating in workshops, or watching documentaries that highlight diverse cultures.
- Empathy and perspective-taking: Encourage individuals to practice empathy by considering the experiences, struggles, and perspectives of people from different racial and cultural backgrounds. Engaging in dialogue with diverse individuals, inside and outside of prison, can develop empathy and broaden their understanding of cultural diversity.
- Cultural sensitivity training: Offer programs to help individuals understand and appreciate different cultural norms, values, traditions, and communication styles. These

programs can provide insights into different racial and ethnic backgrounds, promoting empathy and understanding.

- Peer support and mentoring: Foster an environment that encourages positive interactions between individuals from different racial backgrounds. Establishing peer support groups or mentorship programs can provide opportunities to learn from others with diverse experiences and develop understanding.
- Community integration programs: Collaborate with community organizations that focus on diversity and inclusion to provide integration programs upon release. These programs can facilitate connections with members of different cultural communities, creating opportunities for interaction and understanding.
- Diverse social networks: Encourage individuals to actively seek relationships and friendships with individuals from different racial and ethnic backgrounds. Engaging in diverse social networks can help break down stereotypes and biases while fostering an appreciation for cultural differences.
- Conflict resolution and communication skills: Provide training on conflict resolution and effective communication to equip individuals with the tools to address conflicts and misunderstandings that may arise from cultural differences. These skills can help them navigate difficult situations and promote understanding.
- Leadership and advocacy: Encourage individuals to become leaders and advocates for diversity and inclusion by participating in community initiatives and programs that promote cultural understanding. This can empower individuals to actively promote appreciation for diversity inside and outside prison.

Remember that cultivating an appreciation for cultural differences and diversity is an ongoing process that requires continuous learning and personal growth. By providing support, education, and opportunities for interaction, individuals can develop the skills and mindset necessary to appreciate and value cultural diversity upon reentry to society.

From my experience, once you get to know someone, you will discover you have more in common than you thought. The things you value in life are very similar. You may look different on the outside, but what counts is what is on the inside. Most people want a good life and want to do good things. They want to make a difference in their life and family. How about starting there?

X-Cultural Competencies Self-Assessment Questions

Questions	Responses
Review the homework assignment from the last session.	
How culturally competent do you feel?	
What are your concerns about being released and with people of different races and backgrounds?	
What biases do you have?	
How can you overcome them?	

X-Cultural Competencies Mentor Questions

Questions to ask the mentee:	Write out the mentee's responses.
Review the homework assignments from the last session.	
How culturally competent do you feel?	
What are your concerns about being released and with people of different races and backgrounds?	
What biases do you have?	
How can you overcome them?	
Assignment for next week:	
How are the daily behavior questions going?	

Y IS FOR YOUR NETWORK

> *Therefore, encourage one another and build each other up, just as in the fact you are doing.*
> —1 Thessalonians 5:11

What is networking? Networking is where you develop business relationships, share information, and assist each other, personally and professionally. What is significant about building a network? Building a strong professional network is part of enhancing your career and business strategy. People in your network can give you advice. Determine what your purpose is and with whom you want to interact. Not all events are going to be right for you. Be selective in your choices. Choose wisely when adding connections through LinkedIn, which is distinct from Facebook or other social media options. Stay in touch with your LinkedIn network colleagues to maintain an active network without an agenda. LinkedIn makes it very easy to stay in touch. I like to think of social media this way: LinkedIn is for business. Facebook is for friends. Twitter is for purpose, and YouTube is for subscribers.

How do I network? Think about whom you know. In one discussion I had with a gentleman who had been in prison, he took every opportunity to build these relationships. He started with his teachers and staff in prison. Once released, he networked with his parole officer, minister, and friends. In no time at all, he had a job. He is not unusual. Life is what you make of it.

Start by asking them questions. Provide value, not what you want. This is not speed dating. Repeat their name. Make a note on the back of the card of when and where you met them. Follow up within twenty-four hours with an email so they have a memory of you. Do not wait to do this. The goal is to connect. Over time, you will build strong, trusting relationships. Create a win-win relationship. The more often you do this, the more confident you become.

Your network is the golden ticket to career success only if you stay in touch and build strong relationships. Look for opportunities to connect and help people in your network instead of making it all about you. Check in with them periodically to see how they are doing, what they might need, and how you might help. You will feel great when you get to help others in your network. One day, they might be willing to help, mentor, or endorse you.

Inc. Magazine featured an excellent article on networking called "Eight Things Power Networkers Do to Make Connections" by Minda Zetlin. Check it out at https://www.inc.com/minda-zetlin/8-things-power-networkers-do-make-connections.html.

REFERENCES

LinkedIn. https://www.linkedin.com/feed/.

Zetlin, M. "Eight Things Power Networkers Do to Make Connections." https://www.inc.com/minda-zetlin/8-things-power-networkers-do-make-connections.html.

Your Network Self-Assessment Questions

Questions	Responses
What is the purpose of networking?	
How can it help your life or career when you are released?	
Do you enjoy networking?	
In what areas of networking do you feel you need assistance?	
In what areas of networking do you excel?	
Before going to prison, what was the last networking or group event you attended?	
What value can you create when networking?	

Your Network Mentor Questions

Questions to ask the mentee:	Write out the mentee's responses.
What networking events have you attended?	
Describe how you feel when you go to a networking or group event.	
Do you typically go alone to these events or bring someone with you?	
In what areas of networking do you feel you excel?	
In what areas of networking do you need assistance with now?	
Is there a networking event that you are interested in attending when you are released?	
What is stopping you?	
How can I support your growth in this area?	
Assignment for next week:	**Reading for next week:** List out everyone in your network.
How are the daily behavior questions going?	

Z IS FOR ZEALOUS

> *Never be lacking in zeal, but keep your spiritual fervor, serving the Lord.*
> —Romans 12:11

It is time to put it all together and develop the post-release plan with your mentor. Approach life with a zealous perspective and keep Christ at the center of everything you do with daily prayer and meditation. How have you learned and grown with your mentor through the journey so far?

Mentee questions

Complete the A-to-Z Self-Assessment.	
What chapter made the most significant impact on you?	
What have you learned from your mentor?	
How much have you learned?	
Assignment for next week:	
How have the daily behavior questions supported you?	

Mentor questions

Complete the A-to-Z Self-Assessment.	
What chapter made the most significant impact on you?	
What have you learned from your mentor?	
How much have you learned?	
Assignment for next week:	
How have the daily behavior questions supported you?	

Self-Assessment Inventory

ABCs from Prison to Possibility	Now that you have completed the program rate yourself from 1 to 10, 1 being poor and 10 being excellent.	What are you proud of? What is next for you?
A is for *attitude*. Show a positive attitude.		
B is for *behavior*. What behavior do you want to work on first?		
C is for *communication*. Be a good communicator.		
D is for *decision-making*. Improve your decision-making skills.		
E is for *emotional intelligence*. Can you keep your emotions under control?		
F is for *finance*. Become skilled at handling your money.		
G is for *goal setting*. Focus on the most important goals.		
H is for *health*. What is the current state of your health and well-being?		
I is for *integrity*. Maintain your word to yourself and others. Can others trust you 100 percent?		
J is for *Jesus*. Stand up for what you believe in.		
K is for *knowledgeable*. Expand your knowledge base.		
L is for *lifelong learning*. Hold yourself accountable for lifelong learning.		
M is for *mindset*. Explore. Do you like learning from your mistakes?		

ABCs from Prison to Possibility	Now that you have completed the program rate yourself from 1 to 10, 1 being poor and 10 being excellent.	What are you proud of? What is next for you?
N is for *new-media literacy*. Are you skilled in using new media?		
O is for *opportunity*. Actively look for new life opportunities and take appropriate and legal risks.		
P is for *PTSD* (post-traumatic stress disorder). Understand your triggers and learn strategies that work.		
Q is for *questioning*. Become more curious by asking questions.		
R is for *resiliency*. Do you adapt or give up?		
S is for *self-awareness*. Increase your self-awareness.		
Thank you. Show thankfulness and gratitude.		
U is for *understanding*. Learn to listen to others' points of view before sharing yours.		
V is for *victory*. Do you celebrate victories for yourself and others?		
W is for *work*. How strong is your work ethic?		
X—*cultural competency*. Appreciate and respect differences in other races and cultures.		
Y is for *your network*. Work with others and build your support group.		
Z is for *zealous*. Expand opportunities for bringing enthusiasm to your life.		

RELEASE PLANNING FOR SUCCESSFUL REENTRY

Without a reentry plan, you may see no other option than going back to illegal activities. You must prepare for access to food, transportation, clothing, shelter, personal-identification documents, and much more. Working with your mentor, develop a plan for post-release.

According to the Urban Institute Justice Policy Center in Washington, DC, you need to plan for needs, and here are their recommendations (2008):

- *Transportation.* Find out if the prison provides transportation upon release or if you must make the arrangements.
- *Clothing, food, and amenities.* You will have clothes to leave the prison and hopefully basic toiletries. You will need a list of information accessing food resources.
- *Financial resources.* You will receive a nominal amount of money at release time. In Texas, it is $100 unless you are on parole; you will receive an additional $100 when you meet with your parole officer for the first time. Every state varies, so find out.
- *Documentation.* You will need to obtain a state-issued identification card.
- *Housing.* You will need to decide on where to stay post-release. The prison might be able to provide a list of resources and where beds are available. If you are considering returning to your hometown, make sure it is not the place that created the environment for crime. If you return to that place, you certainly will return to prison sooner rather than later.
- *Employment and education.* Ensure you have the appropriate forms and referrals for finding and keeping a job. Ensure you have copies of any completion certificate of education, training, or certifications you participated in.
- *Health care.* Depending on your mental and physical well-being, have a list of programs and contact information you can access post-release.
- *Support systems.* Make sure you obtain a handbook of community resources. Contact family or friends and notify them of your release date and plan.

Each person released from prison will have unique circumstances based on the crime. Another distinction is how an inmate is released, whether it is a supervised or unsupervised release.

Finally, women who get caught up in the criminal justice system and have extensive histories of drug abuse are likely to be clinically depressed, have low self-esteem, have fewer job skills than their male counterparts, tend to be homeless, and have problems with intimate partners (LaVigne et al. 2008, 30). For women working with mentors, develop a post-release plan focusing on employment readiness, housing, and family reunification.

The final steps in developing your release plan: What do you need? What do you have?

Checklist for Integration

Item	Completed: Place an (X) in the row.	Need to obtain: Place an (X) in the row.	Plan/Timeline
☐ Social Security number			
☐ State ID			
☐ Birth certificate			
☐ Copy of release stipulations/rules			
☐ Driver's license			
☐ Transportation determined: family member, friend, or public transportation—cost, routes, etc.			
☐ Housing located: family, friends, halfway house, shelter (include cost)			
☐ Mailing address/receiving documents/organizational folder			
☐ Library card (libraries provide internet access)			
☐ Email address			
☐ Phone/internet			
☐ Educational credentials/transcript requests			
☐ Résumé			
☐ Personal incarceration statement			
☐ Professional clothing—Dress for Success, Goodwill, or your church			
☐ Employment: job or signed employment release			
☐ Access to food: food pantry/shelter			
☐ Budget			
☐ Support groups (VA, PTSD, NAMI, etc.)			

Item	Completed: Place an (X) in the row.	Need to obtain: Place an (X) in the row.	Plan/Timeline
☐ Substance abuse support (NA, AA, etc.)			
☐ Spiritual/church home			
☐ Counseling support			
☐ Health care			
☐ Healthy parenting classes			
☐ Healthy recreational opportunities			
☐ Exercise			
☐ Voting impact of your crime			
☐ Check-ins with parole/probation officer			
☐ Nearest bank/bank account			
☐ Reconnecting with family and children			
☐ Changes in society since incarceration			
☐ Warrant clearance cleanup/criminal record check			
☐ Daily schedule and routines to follow			
☐ Court dates/debts			
☐ Knowing the legal consequences of your conviction			
☐ Trusted advisor/post-release mentor			
☐ Maintaining the daily questions to improve your behavior and choices			
☐ List of resources available in your hometown			

For veterans, the local VA hospital provides various services and programs to support you.

PLAN FOR POST-RELEASE

Career Development Tools

One effective way to get started is by filling out a job application to allow you to know what information you need before creating a résumé. You can complete this and take it when filling out a real job application.

	Company Name

Employment Application (for inmate mentee)

Applicant Information

Full Name: _____ Date: _____
          Last   *First*   *M.I.*

Address: _____
          Street Address   *Apartment/Unit #*

_____
         City   *State*   *ZIP Code*

Phone: _____ Email _____

Date Available: _____ Social Security No.: _____ Desired Salary: $ _____

Position Applied for: _____

Are you a citizen of the United States?   YES ☐   NO ☐   If no, are you authorized to work in the U.S.?   YES ☐   NO ☐

Have you ever worked for this company?   YES ☐   NO ☐   If yes, when? _____

Have you ever been convicted of a felony?

YES ☐   NO ☐

If yes, explain: _____

Education

High School: _____ Address: _____

From: _____ To: _____ Did you graduate? YES ☐ NO ☐   Diploma: _____

College: _____ Address: _____

From: _____ To: _____ Did you graduate? YES ☐ NO ☐   Degree: _____

Other: _____ Address: _____

From: _____ To: _____ Did you graduate? YES ☐ NO ☐   Degree: _____

References

Please list three professional references.

Full Name: _____   Relationship: _____

Company: _____   Phone: _____

Address: _____

Full Name: _____   Relationship: _____

Company: _____   Phone: _____

Address: _____

Full Name: _____   Relationship: _____

Company: _____   Phone: _____

Address: _____

Previous Employment (Begin with most recent employment)

Company: _____ Phone: _____

Address: _____ Supervisor: _____

Job Title: _____ Starting Salary: $_____ Ending Salary: $_____

Responsibilities: _____

From: _____ To: _____ Reason for Leaving: _____

May we contact your previous supervisor for a reference? YES ☐ NO ☐

_____

_____

Company: _____ Phone: _____

Address: _____ Supervisor: _____

Job Title: _____ Starting Salary: $_____ Ending Salary: $_____

Responsibilities: _____

From: _____ To: _____ Reason for Leaving: _____

May we contact your previous supervisor for a reference? YES ☐ NO ☐

_____

_____

Company: _____ Phone: _____

Address: _____ Supervisor: _____

Job Title: _____ Starting Salary: $_____ Ending Salary: $_____

Responsibilities: _____

From: _____ To: _____ Reason for Leaving: _____

May we contact your previous supervisor for a reference?

YES ☐   NO ☐

_____

_____

Military Service

Branch:_____ From: _____ To: _____

Rank at Discharge: _____ Type of Discharge: _____

If other than honorable, explain: _____

Disclaimer and Signature

I certify that my answers are true and complete to the best of my knowledge.
If this application leads to employment, I understand that false or misleading information in my application or interview may result in my release.

Signature: _____ Date: _____

These are activity worksheets that will help you get started in creating a résumé.

Functional Résumé

For adults in transition, the recommended format for creating a résumé is the functional résumé. In a functional résumé, you do not list the years of employment, which will allow you some flexibility, and you later explain any gaps in the interview. To prepare for this, think about jobs you might like to apply for (list them below):

What is your job objective?

My job objective is:

_____

What skills are needed for this job?

What education is needed for this job?

What experience is needed for this job?

What skills and abilities do you have for this job? Where are the gaps?

Now let's discover all the things you have accomplished in your life so far:

- What problems have you solved?
- What responsibilities have you taken on?
- Have you been promoted in prison or received a certificate?
- What differences have you made, and what are the reasons they matter?

Describe some of your achievements. Use action verbs (examples include *manage, communicate, research, design, teach, help*, etc.).

List your work history:

Work History

Title of the Job (List most recent first)	Duties	City, State
Title of the Job	Duties	City, State
Title of the Job	Duties	City, State

Education and Training

List your education, training, and certifications.

Education	Training	Certifications

What was the name of the degree, and where was it completed (school, city, and state)?

Summary Statement of Key Points

List some of the soft skills you possess, such as excellent communication skills, outstanding customer service skills, being adaptable, team player, punctuality, etc.

Sample Résumé

KATHLEEN JONES

CONTACT

example@example.com

555-555-5555

123 Main Street,
San Francisco, CA 94122

EDUCATION

2009

**Bachelor of Arts - Early
Childhood Educatio**

San Francisco, CA

SKILLS

- Personnel records maintenance
- New hire orientation
- Administrative skills
- Compensation/payroll
- Hiring and retention
- Benefits administration
- HRIS applications proficient
- Policies implementation

PROFESSIONAL SUMMARY

Experienced HR professional with a bachelor's degree in Early
Childhood Education and a passion for working with children and their
families. Organized, personable, and action-oriented with a strong
ability to communicate efficiently.

WORK EXPERIENCE

HR/Accouting Assistant
Dancor Solutions | San Francisco, CA

1/2004 - 10/2012
- Client facing interaction with leading Central Ohio business including Bath and Body Works, Coach, Lane Bryant, Value City Furniture, and Victoria's Secret.
- Supported accounting functions, including accounts payable and receivable.
- Developed and implemented company HR procedures that included the employee handbook, employee benefits, disciplinary measures, and performance reviews.
- Organized company events with multiple vendors for 100+ guests.
- Managed executive calendars and travel.
- Developed onboarding protocols and trained new company employees.

HR Assistant
Macy's | San Francisco, CA

2/1/2002 - 11/2004
- Promoted from part-time seasonal employee to full-time within 6 months.
- Responsible for screening and job placement for applicants.
- Implemented new employee training courses.
- Supported accounting functions including payroll.
- Organized large company events with multiple vendors for 100+ guests.

Drafting Your Résumé

Now that you have worked through all the parts of the résumé, it is time to write your own.

Sample

Name Email Address Phone Number
Objective:
Summary of Qualifications
Relevant Experience
Work History
Education/Training Proof of Education/Certifications

Letters of Recommendation/References (Separate Documents)

Make a list of three professional references and three personal references, if possible. Make sure you ask them before listing their names. Keep the list with their complete names, addresses, phone numbers, and email addresses with you. Recommendations can come from a chaplain, pastor, teacher, friend, or past employer.

Professional Reference	Name	Address (City State, Zip Code)	Email Address	Phone Number
1.				
2.				
3.				
Personal Reference	Name	Address (City State, Zip Code)	Email Address	Phone Number
4.				
5.				
6.				

Clothing

Illustrate good and poor examples.

Start preparing what you will wear to the interview and, when hired, what you will wear to work. It should be clean, pressed, conservative, and professional. This may be a struggle for you in the beginning. Organizations like Dress for Success or Goodwill can support you. There are also resale shops. If none of those are available, you might borrow something from a friend, but make sure it is clean and fits.

You might be fortunate enough to work for a company that supplies uniforms, but you need clothing for the interview. Make sure you have a good pair of shoes. You will need work boots in some fields, so keep that in mind when planning.

Personal Hygiene

You only get one chance to make a good first impression. Make sure you bathe, use deodorant, get your nails clipped, comb your hair, shave, put on basic makeup for women, brush, and floss your teeth.

Handshake

Practice your handshake before going to an interview. It should be firm but not hand-crushing. For women, it needs to be firm as well and not weak. This is an important step in making a good impression.

Eye Contact

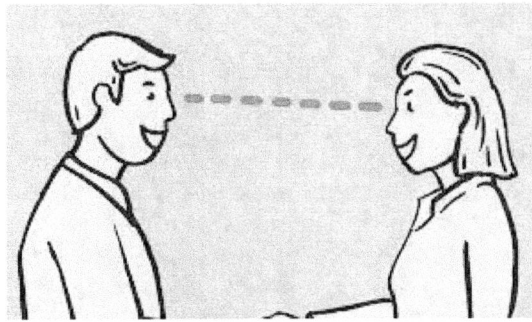

Looking people in the eye when you meet them or during an interview is key to building trust. Do not stare them down but look at them.

Punctuality

Once you get an appointment for an interview, map out how long it will take to get there, depending on your transportation. Give yourself extra time to make it to the interview. It is ideal to arrive fifteen minutes early. Realize that people are watching once you get to the interview and are waiting, so be very professional.

Interviewing

It is now time to prepare for the interview itself. Practice, practice. Be ready to answer the questions clearly and concisely. A typical interviewer might say, "Tell me about yourself." While most people are prepared to discuss their education and skills, behavior-based questions differ slightly. The employer knows that skill sets are transferable. They want to know they are hiring a person with a set of skills that work within their organization.

The Second Chance Center has great resources for interviewing skill development. One of their suggestions is to use "I" statements instead of "you" statements:

I...
- am motivated
- am resourceful
- am a team player

- am even tempered
- follow through
- am dependable

I have a...
- positive attitude
- a lot of energy
- good problem-solving skills

I like...
- variety
- challenges
- learning
- working independently
- working on a team

Now that you have an idea about how to start, write out how you might create a brief statement about yourself.

Warm-Up Activity

Take a few minutes and write out a statement about yourself using this sample as an outline:

> My name is _____. I am a customer service representative with _____ years making people happy. I am a great listener and can assess the customer's needs quickly. I have excellent follow-through. (List your strengths)
>
> I am working on _____ (education or certification here). I participated in the Bridges to Life program (or life-skills training, etc). (Share what programs you have taken advantage of to better yourself. If you are bilingual, mention it here.)

Highlight your most recent accomplishments and close by talking about your professional goal related to this employer.

Interviewing

Interviewing is a skill that can be developed. You only get one chance to make a good first impression. You are interviewing the moment you arrive at the location. Keep your energy up. Dress professionally. Employers want enthusiastic people who show up on time, get along with others, and can communicate. Employers want to hire you, so close out the interview by sharing why you should be hired and saying you would like to work for the organization.

Second Chance Center has a list of ten interview questions and how to respond:

1. Tell me about yourself. (This can be a tricky question. Talk about your highlights [two minutes] and past work experiences. Don't spend twenty minutes telling your life story.)
2. Why should we hire you? (Make sure you discuss how your strengths match the position, not because you need a job or are desperate. This may be true, but you cannot let it show.)
3. What is your greatest strength? What is your greatest weakness?
4. Why do you want to work here?
5. Tell me how your skills are a match for this job.
6. When you were employed, why did you leave your last job?
7. What is your greatest accomplishment?
8. Describe a difficult work situation and what you did to overcome it.
9. Where do you see yourself in five years?
10. Do you have any questions for me?

According to Jobcast by Indeed (October 2, 2020), here are some sample behavior-based questions. This model is called CAR—Circumstance, Action, and Result. Practice how you might answer:

- Tell me about a time when you handled a challenging situation. What happened, and what was the result?
- Tell me about a time when you made a mistake. How did you handle it?
- Tell me about how you work under pressure.
- Give me an example of how you set goals.
- Tell me about a time you were angry and how you handled it. What was the outcome?
- Share an example of how you have helped motivate another person.
- Often at the end of the interview, employers expect you to ask a few questions. Typical questions you might ask are as follows:
  - Can you describe a typical day in this position?
  - To whom will I be reporting?
  - What do you like about working here?
  - What do you find challenging working here?
  - When will you decide, and how will you notify me?

Discussing Criminal History: The Challenging Questions

How do I answer questions about incarceration?

There are many ways to handle this situation. The Second Chance Center recommends five possible approaches. Regardless, write out what you want to share. Practice your response. Don't leave your reply to chance.

1. When applying for a job, you might want to attach a statement about your criminal background and then talk with the hiring manager about the job you are applying for and how you are qualified.
2. In the interview, when asked, "Tell me about yourself," talk about your strengths and how you are a good fit for the job. Add something like, "In addition to these experiences, I would like to take the time to share something more personal about myself" (share your prepared statement).
3. Another way to reveal your past is when the employer asks about your greatest weakness. Give your prepared statement.
4. At the end of the interview, when the employer has finished asking all their questions, and you have asked your questions, say something like, "Before I leave today, there is something I would like you to know." Then tell the employer your prepared statement.
5. Once the interview is over, you did a great job, and they extended an offer; it is time to accept the offer, but you can also disclose to the employer your criminal background. Share with them your prepared statement.

When talking about your criminal background, be honest, but soften the way it is presented.

Examples:
- o I was in possession of a controlled substance.
- o I was using my body as a means of earning a living.
- o I was in a verbal/physical confrontation, and as a result, someone lost their life.
- o I helped someone during a crime that took place.
- o I had unauthorized possession of a firearm.
- o I used my authority/access to take money/property that did not belong to me.

Are-You-Ready Checklist

- ☐ What is your confidence level? Your mindset? Your energy level?
- ☐ Résumé—take a copy for each person interviewing you.
- ☐ Bring two pens – one with blue ink and one with black ink.
- ☐ Bring some note-taking paper (a spiral notebook is an option).
- ☐ Know in advance how to get to the location (give yourself ample time to get there at least fifteen minutes early).
- ☐ Take your driver's license/ID card and Social Security card.

- ☐ Produce your letters of recommendation on good stationery (if asked).
- ☐ Produce your list of references (including complete contact information—name, address, phone number, and email address; include personal and professional references).
- ☐ Research the company in advance—go online.
- ☐ Practice interviewing.
- ☐ Be professionally dressed.
- ☐ Go to the interview alone.
- ☐ Turn off your cell phone. Do not take beverages or food into the interview. Do not smoke or chew gum.
- ☐ Get a good night's sleep the night before.
- ☐ Have a firm handshake, but not too strong.
- ☐ Maintain eye contact.
- ☐ Remember the interviewer's name and ask if you can have their card when you leave.
- ☐ Take only the essentials and be organized.

Networking

Start making a list of people you know who can help you find legal employment. It might be a family member, friend, parole officer, minister, teacher, etc. The job search can be made easier by carefully thinking through your network and communicating to them what you want to accomplish upon release.

LinkedIn

https://www.linkedin.com/

LinkedIn is the best business social media profile presence you can build. You will need an email address, résumé, and professional photo to start. Over time, you can build out the sections. It is also a great way to enhance your professional network.

Job-Search Leads

There are many excellent job boards or employment websites. Some of the most robust are the following:

- Indeed.com (https://www.indeed.com/)
- CareerBuilder.com (https://www.careerbuilder.com/)
- SimplyHired.com (https://www.simplyhired.com/)

Once you have your résumé, you can upload your résumé to these employment sites to help direct your job search.

Cover Letter

While not every job requires a cover letter, it is very important to customize your cover letter for each job you are applying for. You might say that is a lot of work. It does require effort, but it will pay off. You are asking the employer for a job, so think about this. If you spend a few extra minutes customizing this cover letter so you can be hired, it is the equivalent of a year's salary. The answer must be yes; it is worth it!

Now Hired, Now What?

Now that you are hired, what does the employer expect? They expect you to arrive on time, dressed and ready to go. They expect you to be able to do all the things you stated in the interview. They expect you to get along with your peers at work and with management. They will not tolerate no-shows or latecomers. They will not tolerate cussing or violence in the workplace. So, all the work has been done in preparation for release, and working on the soft skills will help you transition back into the workplace.

THINGS THEY DO NOT TELL YOU ABOUT REINTEGRATION: LIFE SKILLS FOR SUCCESS

No one can know your story and what you have been through. It has been a long journey to get to your day of release. You will be filled with many emotions from excitement to anxiety or depression. This will not be easy. For several years, your life has become regulated from when you get up to when you go to bed. Every decision has been made for you—when you eat, when you work, where and when you can walk, when you have free time, etc. The lighting and noise in the units become a way of life.

Walking out of the prison can give you a moment of euphoria. Hopefully, this book has given you a glimpse of things you must prepare for. You will have responsibilities you have not had in years.

If you were incarcerated due to drugs, how will you resist the temptation when you are free? Get into and stay in a program with a sponsor. It is a day-to-day battle. You may need to go to meetings *every day* for support.

Build a relationship with social workers so your transition can be supported. Find a church. Your transition can go in one of two directions—you choose.

Get involved outside with support groups, educational programs, and a church as soon as possible. Get a sponsor, counselor, or mentor for support and accountability. Counseling and other support services are free through agencies such as Court Services and the Offenders Supervision Agency.

Register with community healthcare providers and keep up with all your necessary medications.

Know your purpose and self-worth. Keep God first in all things. Keep your daily questions present.

SUMMARY

We pray that your journey past the prison walls will be successful. We wanted to share inspiring quotes for you to refer to when life becomes challenging, and your fears become present.

"Every moment is a fresh beginning." –T. S. Eliot

"In the middle of difficulty lies opportunity." –Albert Einstein

"Remember no one can make you feel inferior without your consent."
–Eleanor Roosevelt

God bless you.

RESOURCES

Angela House, Houston
angelahouse.org

Bexar Country Reentry Roundtable,
San Antonio
gov.bexar.org/reentry

Bridges to Life
https://www.bridgestolife.org/

Birth Certificates
Cdc.gov/nchs/w2w/index.htm

Career Recovery Resources
https://www.careerandrecovery.org/

Celebrate Recovery
https://www.celebraterecovery.com/

Community Re-Entry Network Program, Houston Health Department
houstontxgov/health/CRNP

Dress for Success
https://dressforsuccess.org/

Excel Center
https://www.goodwillcentraltexas.org/excel-center

Forgiven Felons, Dallas
forgivenfelons.org

Food Assistance
www.fns.usda.gov/snap/apply

Free-Man House
Dallasfreemanhouse.org

Goodwill Central of Texas
https://www.goodwillcentraltexas.org/

Houston Community College
https://www.hccs.edu/

Houston Foodbank Serving for Success,
Houston
houstonfoodbank.org

Hope City Church
https://hopecity.com/hchome/

Kairos Ministry
https://www.kairosprisonministry.org/

Magnificat Houses, Houston
mhihouston.org

Mentor -Care Ministries, Bedford
mentorcare.org

Mike Barber Ministries
https://www.mikebarber.org/

MTC Management & Training Corporation
https://www.mtctrains.com/

National Alliance on Mental Illness
https://nami.org/Home

National Center for PTSD
https://www.ptsd.va.gov/

Perpetual Help, Victoria
perpetualhelphome.org

Prison Entrepreneurship Program
https://www.pep.org/

Search Homeless Services, Houston
searchhomeless.org

Ser-Job for Progress, Houston
serhouston.org

Sharing Hope Ministry, Amarillo
sharinghopeministry.org

Spirit Key Ministry, Houston
spiritkey.org

Star of Hope, Houston
sohmission.org

The Bridge, Dallas
bridgenorthtexas.org

Texas Inmate Families Association
Amarillo tifa.org

Texas Inmate Families Association,
Houston
tifa.org

Texas Offenders Reentry Initiative,
Fort Worth
medc-tori.org

Vital Records
usa.gov/topics

Unlocking Doors, Dallas
unlockingdoors.org

Windham School District
https://www.wsdtx.org/

Work-Faith Connection, Houston
workfaithconnection.org

REFERENCES

Anderson. L. and D. Krathwohl. 2001. "Revised Bloom's Taxonomy." https://thesecondprinciple.com/teaching-essentials/beyond-bloom-cognitive-taxonomy-revised/.

"Attitude." 2018. https://www.google.com/search?q=attitude+definition&oq=attitude+&aqs=chrome.5.69i57j35i39j0l4.5240j1j8&sourceid=chrome&ie=UTF-8.

Bloom, B. 1956. "Bloom's Taxonomy." http://www.nwlink.com/~donclark/hrd/bloom.html.

Brown, L. and J. Rohn. 2019. "Why Attitude Is Everything." https://www.youtube.com/watch?v=nbfFDnKkMvw.

Contreras, R. A., (June 2018). A communication guide for ex-offenders. CSUSB Scholarworks. Retrieved on June 30, 2023, from https://scholarworks.lib.csusb.edu/cgi/viewcontent.cgi?article=1765&context=etd

"Communication Skills: How to Improve Communication Skills, 7 Tips." 2018. https://www.youtube.com/watch?v=mPRUNGGORDo.

Dale Carnegie. 2018. https://www.dalecarnegie.com/en/franchise-locations.

Davis, L. M., J. L. Steele, R. Bozick, M. V. Williams, S. Turner, J. N. V. Miles, J. Saunders, and P. S. Steinberg. 2014. "How Effective Is Correctional Education, and Where Do We Go from Here?" Bureau of Justice Assistance. U.S. Department of Justice. RAND Corporation. https://www.rand.org/pubs/research_reports/RR564.html.

Dweck, C. 2009. *Mindset: How We Can Learn to Fulfill Our Potential.* https://www.amazon.com/Mindset-Psychology-Carol-S-Dweck/dp/0345472322/ref=sr_1_1?ie=UTF8&qid=1518884922&sr=8-1&keywords=mindset+by+carol+dweck.

Emmons, R. A. 2004. "The Psychology of Gratitude." https://www.forbes.com/sites/larryalton/2016/09/07/heres-how-sleep-affects-your-day-at-the-office/#3ed1c8e7820b.

"Emotional Intelligence." 2018. https://www.youtube.com/watch?v=Y7m9eNoB3NU/.

Goleman, D. 1995. *Emotional Intelligence: Why It Can Matter More Than IQ.* New York, NY: Bantam Books.

Gordon, J. 2007. "How to Deal with Energy Vampires." http://www.jongordon.com/positive-tip-energy-vampires.

Grammarly. 2018. https://www.grammarly.com.

Hall, K. M. 2021. A guide to PTSD Triggers (and how to cope). Retrieved on June 30, 2023, from https://www.goodrx.com/conditions/ptsd/common-triggers GoodRxHealth

Holmes, L. 2017. "10 Things Grateful People Do Differently." https://www.huffingtonpost.com/entry/habits-of-grateful-people_us_565352a6e4b0d4093a588538.

Jobcast. 2020. "30 Behavioral Interview Questions to Prepare for (with example answers)" (October 2). Indeed. https://www.indeed.com/career-advice/interviewing/most-common-behavioral-interview-questions-and-answers.

Lavigne, N., E. Davies, T. Palmer, and Halberstadt. 2008. "Release Planning for Successful Reentry." https://www.urban.org/sites/default/files/publication/32056/411767-Release-Planning-for-Successful-Reentry.PDF.

Management Mentors. 2018. https://www.management-mentors.com/resources/corporate-mentoring-programs-resources-faqs#Q1.

Maxwell, J. C. 2003. *Attitude 101: What Every Leader Needs to Know*. https://www.amazon.com/Attitude-101-Every-Leader-Needs/dp/0785263500.

Mehrabian, A. 1972. *Nonverbal Communication*. Chicago, Il: Aldine-Atherton.

———. n.d. *Communication Model*. https://www.toolshero.com/communication-skills/communication-model-mehrabian/.

MindTools. (2018). "Improve Your Listening Skills with Active Listening." https://www.youtube.com/watch?v=t2z9mdX1j4A.

National Speakers Association. 2018. https://www.nsaspeaker.org/.

Robbins, M. 2018. "Bring Your Whole Self to Work." https://www.youtube.com/watch?v=bd2WKQWG_Dg.

Sinek, S. 2011. "Start with Why: How Great Leaders Inspire Action." https://www.ted.com/talks/simon_sinek_how_great_leaders_inspire_action.

Small Business Administration (SBA). n. d. https://www.sba.gov/.

Small Business Development Center—Houston. 2019. https://www.sbdc.uh.edu/sbdc/default.asp.

Smith, E. E. 2017. *The Power of Meaning: Crafting a Life That Matters*. New York, NY. Random House.

TedTalks. 2018. https://www.youtube.com/channel/UCAuUUnT6oDeKwE6v1NGQxug.

"The Attitude Test." 2019. https://www.3smartcubes.com/pages/tests/attitudetest/attitudetest_instructions/Online attitude assessments.

The Global Leadership Foundation. 2018. "Emotional Intelligence Test." https://globalleadershipfoundation.com/geit/eitest.html.

Toastmasters International. 2018. https://www.toastmasters.org/.

The Foundation for Critical Thinking. 2018. https://www.criticalthinking.org/.

Vale, Jack. 2019. "An A–Z of the Skills of the Future." https://guild.co/blog/an-a-z-of-the-skills-of-the-future/.